Designing a Successful KM Strategy

A Guide for the Knowledge Management Professional

Stephanie Barnes and Nick Milton

Information Today, Inc.
Medford, New Jersey

Second printing, January 2016

Designing a Successful KM Strategy: A Guide for the Knowledge Management Professional

Library of Congress Cataloging-in-Publication Data

Barnes, Stephanie.
   Designing a successful KM strategy : a guide for the knowledge management professional / Stephanie Barnes and Nick Milton.
      pages cm
   Includes bibliographical references and index.
   ISBN 978-1-57387-510-3
   1. Knowledge management.   2. Organizational learning.   3. Organizational change.   I. Milton, N. J. (Nick J.) II. Title.
   HD30.2.B3643 2014
   658.4'038--dc23

                                                                2014030264

Printed and bound in the United States of America

President and CEO: Thomas H. Hogan, Sr.
Editor-in-Chief and Publisher: John B. Bryans
Project Editor: Anne P. Mintz
Associate Editor: Beverly M. Michaels
Production Manager: Norma J. Neimeister
Indexer: Candace Hyatt

Interior Design by Amnet Systems
Cover Design by Denise M. Erickson

infotoday.com

To knowledge managers everywhere, in every
organization, industry, and sector on every continent.
May all your strategies be successful!

Contents

Figures and Tables

Acknowledgments

Thanks to my co-author, Nick Milton. *Designing a Successful KM Strategy* was his idea and I'm so grateful that he asked me to co-author it with him. I learned a lot working with him, and it has truly enhanced my Knowledge Management knowledge—proving that there is always more to learn! Thanks also to Jane Dysart for connecting me to John Bryans at Information Today, Inc., who was just as excited about this title as Nick and I were. Finally, thank you to everyone who has helped me develop my passion for Knowledge Management, whatever role you played.

—Stephanie Barnes

Thanks to Stephanie Barnes for her hard work and contributions to *Designing a Successful KM Strategy*, and especial thanks to Rod Abson for critically reviewing the manuscript and to Dan Ranta for the Foreword. I would also like to acknowledge all the knowledge managers and business people I have worked with over the years who have contributed to the development of the ideas within the book.

—Nick Milton

Foreword

My most recent experience in Knowledge Management came over a 10-year period with a major global oil and gas company. For this international energy company with thousands of job sites (often quite remote) spread across 30 countries, the challenge of sharing knowledge was very real—and the potential payoff was huge. Facing fierce competition on all fronts, senior managers realized that to continue on its success trajectory, the company needed to rapidly and effectively harness the knowledge of its highly skilled but geographically distributed workforce. Instead of assuming that technology either was the solution or was irrelevant to knowledge management, senior managers understood that effective global Communities of Practice required new processes, roles, cultures, and technologies. Moreover, they recognized that each Community of Practice had to be focused on solving difficult business challenges, and that the entire Knowledge Management program needed to be "based in the business" to be successful in the long run.

Ensuring that each individual Community of Practice has the greatest chance to succeed is a process that begins long before the community is formed. Many authors and consultants stress the informal nature of such communities, arguing that any attempt to systematize them will crush them. We found the exact opposite—that without clear and explicit links to the organizational strategy and its business purpose, communities often evolve in ways that fail to contribute to business goals. We developed two fundamental principles in this regard.

Firstly, no Community of Practice was created without a clear and detailed business case that specified the value proposition to the company; community leaders and members agreed upon this business case. Insisting on a business case prior to the creation of a Community of Practice goes against the typical "let a thousand flowers bloom" approach that is often promoted in the Knowledge Management literature. But in many cases, uncontrolled growth of new communities saps employees' attention and engagement, and leads to neglect and community failure. Setting a strategic goal at the outset means that every potential new community must have a strong business justification, which signals to potential leaders and members that the result will not be something that consumes their time without producing real business value. Community members, in turn, see this phenomenon and this drives a higher level of engagement since most employees have laudable amounts of professional pride.

Proposals for new Communities of Practice also clearly had to specify the kinds of deliverables that would be produced through the ongoing operation of the community, and the specific kinds of activities that the community would be supporting. Deliverables (such as research reports and reusable work products) and activities (such as electronic discussions and teleconferences) needed to relate directly to the business case and support the attainment of business strategy. A high degree of focus on these two areas helped separate the wheat from the chaff, leading new community proponents away from fuzzy "more is better" claims about collaboration and toward specific activities that were likely to produce a solid payoff for the collective investment of time.

Ultimately, managers provided each new Community of Practice—through its business case, its deliverables, and its activities—with a clear operating model that connected it to the overall strategy of the business. Following these two principles had a profound effect on the nature and character of communities at this large global company: it aligned them with organizational priorities, helped members understand how they can affect important business goals, provided clear justification for why members should invest their time in the community, and shifted the idea of Knowledge Management away from abstract concepts and toward a concrete set of measurable objectives. As a result, communities became a cornerstone of this company's strategic ability to reach its business goals and deliver additional value through global collaboration and expertise sharing.

The key to getting any Knowledge Management program off to a promising start from a business value standpoint is to strategically address the Knowledge Management opportunities. Knowledge Management should always start with discovering what the business is interested in accomplishing. This is not just the immediate business group or function grappling with Knowledge Management, but also should include alignment all the way to the top of any organization. Alignment creates the opportunity for purposeful collaboration where value can be created and sustained over time. The challenge is often that organizations cannot easily figure out how to set out on a path to create measurable and sustainable value. Smart managers intuitively understand the importance of the problems that Knowledge Management efforts are often designed to address. However, the lack of strategic awareness often results in poorly organized Knowledge Management efforts that are sprinkled across a decentralized construct and not implemented consistently across an organization to ensure standards and best practices are being leveraged with business value in mind.

To ensure Knowledge Management is strategic and linked to business value, organizations need to ensure there are strong relationships between those in charge of implementing Knowledge Management and business leaders. While smart managers can understand how Knowledge Management can support business issues, they cannot get to an intimate understanding where they are ready to embrace Knowledge Management solutions until the necessary work is done to show the linkage between purposeful collaboration and the solution of critical business issues. Knowledge Management practitioners must be able to employ techniques such as those described within this book, to make the connections between Knowledge Management and business value opportunities. This is where the business relationships come into play since it is only with strong relationships that a Knowledge Management practitioner can convince business leaders to try these and other techniques to make these imperative linkages.

Knowledge Management success requires a commitment by management to actively support collaboration so that employees feel that it is part of their "day jobs" and to ensure a standard means to share with their colleagues. It is possible to design easy and efficient technology-enabled processes that focus on connecting people as part of their daily work, to enable the seamless flow of lessons learned and best practices to the right people at the right time. Showing managers that this approach to knowledge transfer maximizes employees' efforts to solve problems is the key. Any corporate culture will always be particularly sensitive to anything perceived to be an additional burden, and one clear sign of Knowledge Management success is that KM activities are not viewed in this manner.

At this writing, Knowledge Management is "hotter" than ever. Organizations across all sectors and industries are scrambling to figure out how to get more connected workforces. There is ample evidence that a focus on collaboration is a critical enabler for the future of any organization, just as there is ample proof that Knowledge Management—when strategically implemented in alignment with business value—enables organizations to build greater levels of openness and trust, which, in turn, improves employee collaboration and the sharing of valuable best practices and lessons learned. That type of sharing is the heart and soul of Knowledge Management, and the Knowledge Management strategy is the foundation stone for making this happen.

In *Designing a Successful KM Strategy* you will find a straightforward and practical guide to the creation of a clear, simple, and business-focused Knowledge Management strategy. As we found in the oil and gas company described earlier, this is your first step to delivering the huge value that Knowledge Management makes possible.

Dan Ranta

Director, DR Consulting

Introduction

Designing a Successful KM Strategy is designed for you, the knowledge manager, in order to help you develop a strategy for Knowledge Management (KM) that will not only allow you to be successful in implementing KM in your organization, but also give you a solid understanding of why it is important to start with a strategy rather than jumping in without a well thought-out plan.

The introductory chapters describe KM, and share what we believe to be the basic principles behind successful KM implementation, based on our observation of, and involvement in, KM programs over the past 20 years.

Subsequent chapters take each section of our recommended KM strategy structure and explain what they should contain, and provide you with approaches and exercises for creating the relevant component of your own strategy.

The idea of writing a strategy is a simple idea, but don't think for a minute that this will be an easy undertaking. Writing a KM strategy is going to require a lot of thinking, a lot of discussing, a lot of socializing of ideas, and a lot of input from the most senior people in your organization as well as from frontline staff. If done well, it will provide the foundation for a highly successful KM implementation. A good strategy more than repays the time taken to write it.

The process of developing the strategy is summarized in Figure 0.1, and this flowchart can be used as an overview of the contents of *Designing a Successful KM Strategy*.

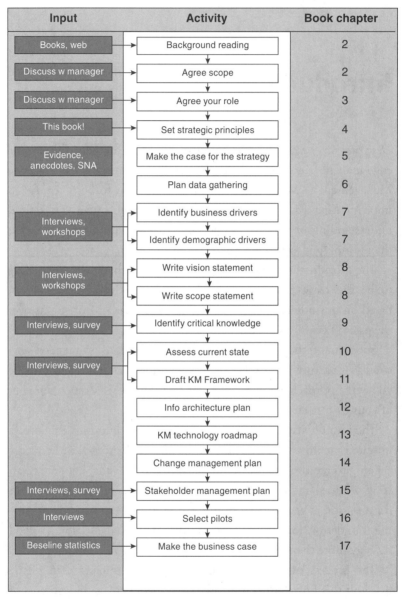

Input	Activity	Book chapter
Books, web	Background reading	2
Discuss w manager	Agree scope	2
Discuss w manager	Agree your role	3
This book!	Set strategic principles	4
Evidence, anecdotes, SNA	Make the case for the strategy	5
	Plan data gathering	6
Interviews, workshops	Identify business drivers	7
	Identify demographic drivers	7
Interviews, workshops	Write vision statement	8
	Write scope statement	8
Interviews, survey	Identify critical knowledge	9
Interviews, survey	Assess current state	10
	Draft KM Framework	11
	Info architecture plan	12
	KM technology roadmap	13
	Change management plan	14
Interviews, survey	Stakeholder management plan	15
Interviews	Select pilots	16
Beseline statistics	Make the business case	17

Figure 0.1   Flow diagram for writing a KM strategy

The Need for Strategy

> *"Strategy without tactics is the slowest route to victory.*
> *Tactics without strategy is the noise before defeat."*
> —Sun Tzu

Anyone interested in the way business works should watch the popular TV program "The Apprentice."[1] This is a reality game show, where teams of young entrepreneurs are given business tasks, then compete against each other to complete the tasks in the most effective way. The losing team will lose one of its members each week—"fired" from the program as the numbers are whittled down to eventually determine the winner. The tasks vary from episode to episode, as do the reasons for the failure of any one team. Analyzing these reasons will provide you with a very instructive primer in how to succeed in business.

The seventh episode of the 2012 UK series threw the issue of business strategy into very sharp focus. The primary task was to buy goods from a warehouse and sell them at a market stall. The team that held the most cash and stock at the end of the day was the winner. One team leader took a very strategic view. His strategy was "stock the items that sell the best, and where demand is greatest." Quickly he determined the key item that sold well and delivered a good margin (it was a slightly tacky-looking bottle of self-applied fake tan lotion), and set about acquiring as much stock of this product as he possibly could. The other team was project-managed by a young woman with huge levels of energy and enthusiasm, and excellent selling skills, but who had little time for strategy. Instead she reacted tactically to what was on the warehouse shelves, and spread her resources around several products. Not surprisingly, the strategic leader won the task, and the tactical leader lost. The tactical team was good at selling, but to paraphrase Sun Tzu, its sales tactics were just the noise before defeat.

What if, instead of selling fake tan lotion at a market stall, you were implementing KM in an organization? Do you still need a strategy?

Of course you do. You may not be in a reality game show, but you are in a competitive situation. You are in competition for internal resources and internal attention. If you do not have a good strategy then good tactics are not going to save you. You should not be in the position of responding tactically to items on the "KM warehouse shelves," rather, you should know what your business needs KM to deliver and focus on where the demand is greatest. We are constantly hearing of yet another KM program closed, and yet another knowledge manager looking for a job, as the company sought to cut back on spending. If you are not seen to be addressing the firm's crucial operational issues and supporting its strategy, then you may be viewed as optional, and times are too tight for optional expenditures.

It is a commonly stated that 80 percent of KM programs fail. Whether that high failure rate is close to accurate depends on what you mean by "KM program" and how you judge failure; that said, there certainly have been many failed KM programs. Some of the common reasons for failure include:

- KM is not introduced with an operational focus

- KM is not introduced as a change program

- The KM team does not have the right people to deliver change

- The KM team "preaches only to the choir" rather than engaging all the key stakeholders in a managed way

- Only parts of the KM solution are implemented, rather than the entire framework

- KM is never embedded into the organization's processes and activities

- There is no effective high-level sponsorship

A good KM strategy will help you avoid these pitfalls; the chapters in *Designing a Successful KM Strategy* address all of them. A strategy is "the art of distributing and applying means to fulfill the ends;"[2] your KM strategy must make those ends clear, and help you determine and deploy a means to meet those objectives.

Throughout *Designing a Successful KM Strategy* we conclude most of the chapters with an example taken from one of several public-domain KM strategies to illustrate the points we make in that chapter.

What Will a Sound KM Strategy Do for You?

A sound KM strategy will help you define where you are heading, and what the end point should be. The process of defining the vision and the objectives for KM within your organization will require a set of vital scene-setting conversations with business leaders and the development of a common understanding of the value KM can deliver.

Your strategy will provide a set of principles or ground rules to guide your actions, and guide your decision making during KM implementation, in order to create the greatest chance of success and help you avoid the reasons for failure we have already listed.

Your strategy, if it follows the principles mentioned previously, will be closely linked to your organization's objectives, strategy, and results. This will help protect you from being seen as peripheral to the operations, and thus an easy target for downsizing.

Your strategy will form the framework for planning purposes. It will define the areas of focus, the risks to be addressed, and the allies to work with, as well as the areas of greatest risk.

Your strategy will guide you in deciding what not to do. If a tactic is outside the framework, or in opposition with the principles, then it is not strategic but rather a waste of resources.

The strategy also looks at implementation priorities and issues. It is not just a vision; it is a high-level approach to how the vision will be realized.

Your strategy is a public agreement with your leadership. It represents agreed ground rules for KM implementation, and will have leadership's blessing and support. If over time that support wanes then you can go back to the strategy, remind your leaders that it was agreed upon, and claim their support (or renegotiate the strategy). The strategy is a key decision point for the organization.

Your strategy allows you to be flexible in your KM program, but in a managed way. As your organization changes, driven by changes in your organizational priorities or in the competitive or technological landscape, your KM strategy may also need to change, but all changes will need to be renegotiated with your steering group. This is your "Management of Change" process for the KM implementation.

What We Won't Cover

Designing a Successful KM Strategy is a guide to writing a KM strategy tailored to the needs of your organization and to your organizational context. It will not tell you what KM framework you need; that is something you'll design yourself. It will provide the headings, or the overall structure of the framework, but not the details of the content, which will be different for each organization.

Neither will the book attempt to tell you how to implement your strategy. To include detailed guidance on KM implementation would have at least doubled the length of our text, and the details of implementation will vary considerably depending on your organizational size, diversity, and geographic spread. *Designing a Successful KM Strategy* is designed to help you create a foundation for success in KM through helping you craft the best possible strategy. Building on that foundation is something you will need to do yourself.

Let's Get Started

We've now considered the value of strategy, and established that an effective KM strategy, aligned with your organization's larger strategy, is the basis and foundation for the success of your KM initiative. So let's move on to Chapter 1 of *Designing a Successful KM Strategy* and begin our work!

Notes

1. "The Apprentice (UK TV Series)," Wikipedia, http://en.wikipedia.org/wiki/The_Apprentice_(UK_TV_series).
2. B. H. Liddell Hart, *Strategy*. 2nd Revised nd ed. (London: Faber, 1967), 321.

What Exactly Is Knowledge Management, and Why Do We Need It?

As a knowledge manager, you are probably beginning to realize that you have a job within a very poorly-defined field. When two or three people talk about Knowledge Management (KM), they often have completely different understandings of what the term means, and therefore what KM will look like in an organization.

One of your first tasks will be to understand both what your manager thinks KM is (and therefore what your job is), and also what aspects of KM will add most value to your organization, even if this is not exactly what your boss had in mind.

A brief mapping of the many fields covered by the term Knowledge Management follows.

The KM Landscape

Let us start down at the data end, where the KM landscape meets the border with data management. Areas of data management which are sometimes referred to as KM include the combination of data through *linked data,* and looking for the patterns within data, through *data mining*, so that new insights can be gained. Where this is applied to customer data or business data, then we get into the analogous disciplines of *CRM* and *Business Intelligence,* which often support organizational learning and decision-making and in that context may fit into your KM strategy.

Next to data comes information, where KM may be involved in several ways. For example, the structuring of information, through *taxonomies, ontologies, folksonomies,* or *information tagging (also known as metadata);* also the retrieval of information, where KM encompasses *enterprise search,* and/or *semantic search;* or the presentation of information, through *intranets,* or *portals,* supported by *content management.* The presentation of information, as well as the creation of explicit "knowledge objects" is an important component of *call center KM,* closely allied to the creation of *customer knowledge bases,* and *knowledge based engineering* is a discipline where engineering design is done based on knowledge models.

The creation of explicit knowledge is a significant part of the KM world, containing many shades of its own. *Knowledge retention* deals with capture of knowledge from retiring staff (also known as *knowledge harvesting*—a retention-based strategy is discussed in Chapter 18), while *lessons capture* and *lesson learning* deal with learning from projects, as do *learning histories* based on multiple interviews.

Another part of the landscape is the *organizational learning* corner. This abuts the border with learning and development, but is concerned with learning of the organization, rather than learning of the individual. In this part of the KM world we find *action learning, business-driven action learning,* and analogous disciplines such as *elearning, coaching,* and *mentoring.*

Organizational learning is related to the area of knowledge transfer, where KM covers the transfer of knowledge through discussion between individuals and teams. This part of KM contains dialogue-based processes such as *peer assist, knowledge handover, knowledge café, baton-passing, after-action review,* and *appreciative inquiry*—processes that are focused on knowledge, but are closely allied to other organizational development methods. Next to this area lies the area of *internal communications,* and (in the case of organizations that create knowledge for others, such as education bodies or development sector organizations) *external communications.*

Knowledge transfer between people—the tacit area, sometimes referred to as *experience management*—takes us into the area of networking. Here we find the *communities of practice*, the *centers of excellence*, the *communities of interest*, and the *social networks*. The latter, of course, are closely allied to *social media*—social media being the technology that supports social networks. Then we have *storytelling*, as a means of knowledge transfer, *crowdsourcing*, as a means of accessing knowledge from a wide source, and *collaboration* as a sort of catch-all term (supported by *collaborative technology*).

There is a whole *innovation* area to KM as well—*open innovation, creativity, deep dives,* and so on—as well as the use of other KM activities previously mentioned to make linkages and expose knowledge to people who will build on it to make new knowledge, products, and services.

Then finally we have the psychological end of KM, where we have disciplines such as *epistemology, sense-making, complexity theory, decision-making theory*, and the part of KM that deals with the lone worker: *personal KM.*

This is a complex landscape covering many different areas, and can be confusing to navigate. As a knowledge manager, however, you need to address enough of the KM landscape that you can put together a framework that is sufficiently complete to add business value to your organization, while not biting off more than you can chew. Hence the need to get clear, with your manager, in regard to how much of this landscape you intend to cover in your KM implementation, and thereby to define the scope of your KM strategy.

The Boston Square that follows may be helpful in that discussion.

A Useful Boston Square

Boston Squares are great. They are a way of taking apart a complex topic; dividing it up using two separate axes to see if the consequent subdivision yields any insight. Boston Squares are the management analyst's dissection tool.

The Boston Square in Figure 1.1 is one you may find useful when considering the scope of KM in your organization. This Boston Square

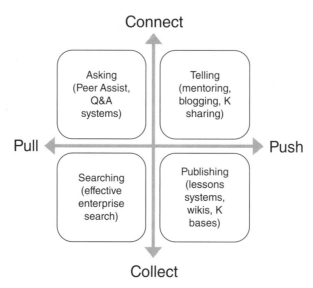

Figure 1.1   Four quadrants of Knowledge Management

divides KM along two dimensions—Connect and Collect (where "Connect" focuses on Connecting people, "Collect" on Collecting content), and Push and Pull (where "Push" is volunteering knowledge, and "Pull" is seeking knowledge). We think the interesting thing about this set of quadrants is that they represent the four poles of KM, each one of which is important. To leave any of these out is to seriously weaken your knowledge strategy and leave holes in your KM framework. As you discuss the scope of your KM implementation with your boss make sure you cover all of the quadrants.

As Figure 1.1 shows, the interplay of connect/collect and push/pull defines four quadrants, which can represent four elements of KM which need to be addressed in your strategy and framework.

Connection and Pull

The pull/connection quadrant is where you address systems, processes and behaviors that support people seeking knowledge from other people. This is the "Asking" quadrant. In many ways, asking is the most effective way of transferring knowledge, and studies show that if people are looking for knowledge, most of the time they will ask (although some recent studies suggest that this is no longer the case for new graduates, for whom a search engine is the first knowledge resource to turn to). Shell, in its KM strategy in the late 1990s, focused primarily on the Asking quadrant. Here you will find technologies such as community discussion forums, Q&A forums, and Yellow Pages, and processes such as peer assist and appreciative inquiry.

Connection and Push

The push/connection quadrant is where you address systems, processes and behaviors that support people sharing their knowledge directly to other people. This is the "Telling" quadrant. Telling is less effective than Asking, but is still a key component of KM. In this quadrant you will find technologies such as blogs and microblogs, and processes such as baton-passing, knowledge handover, mentoring, teaching and lectures.

Collection and Push

The push/collection quadrant is where you address systems, processes and behaviors that support people *contributing* their knowledge to some form of organizational knowledge base. This is the "Publishing" quadrant. In this quadrant you will find technologies such as lessons management systems, repositories for best practices, wikis, call center knowledge bases, Intranets and online libraries. For many, this quadrant is what they immediately think of when they hear the term "KM."

Collection and Pull

The pull/collection quadrant is where you address systems, processes and behaviors which support people *searching* for knowledge on the online systems. In this quadrant you will primarily find the technologies for effective search, whether this is simple search, semantic search, data mining, or text mining.

A Comprehensive Approach

Your KM scope needs to address all four quadrants. There is no point in publishing without search, for example, just as there is no point in searching if that knowledge had not been collected in the first place. Similarly there is no point in focusing purely on tacit knowledge, or purely on explicit knowledge, because both types of knowledge are valuable.

We have, however, seen many organizations that fall into the trap of focusing exclusively on one quadrant. They buy a microblogging tool, for example, and expect it to deliver KM all on its own. Or they focus on wikis and blogs (both within the push quadrant) and find that lots of knowledge is published, but very little used. Or they invest in state-of-the-art search technology, but find that the key knowledge has never been captured in the first place.

Early in 2013 we met with a company that had taken a popular approach to KM; the approach of Collection and Push, which involves making it easy, and expected, for people to Publish. However they had taken it to extremes, and as a result destroyed the value they had hoped to create. This company had introduced multiple ways to publish knowledge (case studies, blogs, wikis, email forums, microblogging) and multiple ways to encourage publishing (reward systems, promotional posters, and the example of senior managers and peers), but only had one system for seeking for knowledge, which was not promoted, rewarded, or used by senior management. As a result, the company staff created a vast supply of published material, much of it duplicated, and none of it well structured, and have almost no demand for that material. Very little of it is being reused, and the huge investment in time and effort publishing material has no business benefit.

The company had focused entirely on Collection and Push, and ended up with an unbalanced KM approach, which delivered no value. Collection and Push is such a popular first-pass approach to KM strategy, with many companies starting from a position of "our strategy is to introduce a knowledge sharing culture" or "we intend to lower the barriers for publication" that it is worth looking at examples like the one previously mentioned, to see what happens when other elements of KM are neglected.

Do not fall into this trap! Instead of a strategy of "creating a knowledge sharing culture," it is better to create a culture where knowledge sharing is balanced with knowledge seeking and knowledge reuse, and supply of knowledge is balanced with demand.

Defining Your Scope

So what do we learn from all this? Is there a conclusion to draw?

We recommend you recognize that KM is a broad and multifaceted field, which presents you with two risks: the risk of trying to do too much, and the risk of doing too little. You need to address enough elements of KM to create a complete framework, while not trying to cover the entire landscape. Use our Boston Square, have a conversation with your manager about what the KM scope might look like, and develop an understanding of the scope your strategy document will need to cover. This is further discussed in Chapter 7. Ultimately, however, you will need to be led by the business need for KM, and to introduce a system that meets this need. This is further discussed in Chapter 6.

Why is KM Needed Now?

A complete discussion of the business drivers for KM appears in Chapter 6, but for now, here are the basics of why we need KM in the early 21st century.

Learning at the Speed of Change

The pace of change and new knowledge creation is incredible, people no longer stay in one job for life, they choose to move around or they are laid-off and get a new job somewhere else. Knowledge does not stay in one place.

We live in a time of rapid demographic change. In Western engineering-based companies, the baby-boomers are retiring and taking decades of hard-won knowledge with them. NASA has already discovered this the hard way—much of the knowledge of the original moon landings has now been lost, as it was never fully captured and so vanished as the Apollo engineers retired. The transfer of baby-boomer knowledge is becoming a critical survival factor for many industries.

At the same time, in the growth economies of the Far East and the Middle East, organizations are seeking to scale up and disseminate knowledge, previously held by few experts, into the heads of a young and expanding workforce. They are seeking to be able to do the same tasks with young staff that were previously done by experienced staff.

The accelerating pace of change makes KM vital. Every organization must learn fast enough to keep up with the pace of change. They must create, improve, and deploy new knowledge, and delete the old knowledge, in order to survive. Your KM strategy must support that speed of learning, and enable every decision maker in the company, no matter what their level; to have access to the knowledge they need, at the time that they need it, in a completely up to date form.

Larry Prusak, a guru of KM, asserted that the only sustainable competitive advantage is what you know, using what you know, and how quickly you can know something new.

Information Overload

We live in an age of information overload, partly because of the availability of technology and the information it allows us to access, and partly because technology has reduced or eliminated the barriers to entry. This has allowed everyone to be a publisher, creating their own information to be shared with the world. Technology helped to create the problem but it can also be used to solve the problem.

As companies and economies become increasingly globalized, there is an increasing need to act collectively and to collaborate across geographies. Knowledge that was held locally now needs to be shared globally. The combination of increased change and increased collectivity makes KM an essential enabler for companies, allowing them to keep up with the pace of change, across global operations. This is shown in Figure 1.2, based on a figure from Blackler (1995).[1]

One of the biggest benefits of any KM system is making knowledge and experience available to the rest of the organization. Whether we are talking about expertise location, lessons learned, peer assist, communities of practice, collaboration, knowledge assets, or any other KM approach, they all make knowledge available to improve consistency

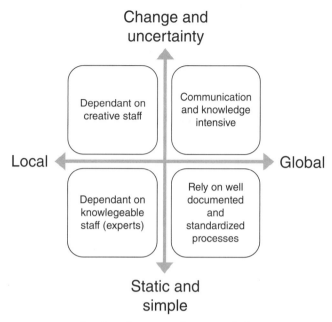

Figure 1.2   Organizational context for Knowledge Management

and standardization in processes, and to enhance decision-making. This results in staff delivering better quality products and services, as they are not reinventing the wheel every time they have to do something, and in staff developing, sharing, reusing, and continuously improving practices across the entire sphere of operations and in pace with the changing business environment.

Summary and Next Steps

KM is a wide field, covering many different sub-topics, not all of which will be relevant to you in your organization. You need to make sure you know which parts of KM are relevant and valuable to the work that you have been asked to do, and you also need to be sure that you cover enough of the KM topic to provide a complete solution. The Boston Square presented previously will help you ensure you cover Connect and Collect, and Push and Pull. Once you are clear on your KM scope, and believe that it is wide enough to cover the Boston Square, but not so wide that you will never complete the task, then you can move on to Chapter 2, where we will begin to clarify the role that you yourself will play.

Note

1.   F. Blackler, "Knowledge, Knowledge Work and Organizations: An Overview and Interpretation," *Organization Studies* 6 (1995): 1021-46.

The Knowledge Manager Role

If you bought, downloaded, borrowed or otherwise acquired *Designing a Successful KM Strategy*, then we will assume you are working as a knowledge manager, or a related role.

But what exactly *is* a knowledge manager? First, as is true of "Knowledge Management," or "KM," it's an elastic term. It can describe a content manager working on a small corner of an intranet, a senior manager driving knowledge-related change in a global enterprise, or any role in between.

If you are drafting a strategy, however, we can assume you have the freedom, at your level in the organization, to influence the way knowledge is treated as a resource; how it is transferred, reused, captured, shared, sought, applied, codified, and otherwise handled in your part of the business. You are accountable for "making KM work" in some if not all areas of the organization.

Perhaps you are a knowledge manager within a project, accountable for ensuring knowledge is treated as a project resource, and that the project acquires the knowledge it needs, and creates the knowledge that other projects and other parts of the business need. Or perhaps you are a knowledge manager for a department, accountable for ensuring that the staff within the department seek, use, create and share knowledge. Or perhaps you are a knowledge manager for an entire organization, looking to define, implement and operate a KM framework across a global enterprise.

In each case you need to look at Knowledge Management strategically, and decide how it will best support the part of the business that lies within your scope. For your part of the business, you are a KM leader.

Key Elements of the KM Leadership Role

We can summarize the main elements of this KM leadership role as follows. In your particular case, some of these elements may need to be expanded beyond this generic content, but all elements of this content should be somewhere in your role description.

- Development of KM strategy. Whichever level you work at, you will need to create a strategy. It could be a KM strategy at project level, or at department level, divisional level, business stream level, or organizational level. The principles are the same though the scale differs.

- Management of a KM framework. The KM framework (described in detail in Chapter 10) is the combination of roles, processes, technology and governance which together describe the means for managing knowledge. If no framework exists, your role will be to design and implement one. If a framework is already in place, your role will be to monitor how it is used, to improve it if needed, and to make sure it is applied effectively.

- Promotion of KM behaviors and culture. Part of implementing KM is to ensure that KM behaviors become the norm in your organization, thus influencing culture change. The behaviors will be driven partly by the framework, which, when embedded into the work structure, will prompt people to "push and pull" and to "connect and collect." Your role is to champion the application of the framework, and to keep KM in people's awareness until it becomes "part of the way we work."

- Measurement and reporting of KM. Your managers will be interested in whether the KM strategy is being applied, whether the framework is operating as expected, and whether KM is delivering the anticipated benefits. An important part of your role is to measure, monitor and report.

Defining the Knowledge Manager

What follows is a role description for a knowledge manager from Samsung SDS.[1] In this role description, we can see the four elements listed above. The first bullet covers development of strategy, bullets two through five cover management of elements of the framework, bullet six addresses culture and bullet seven addresses measurement and reporting.

- Development of KM Strategy. Performs the task of establishing the direction and strategy of KM activities by analyzing an enterprise's management strategy and employees' knowledge requests and planning KM programs.

- Management of Openplace Planning and Operation. Plans/ operates/evaluates/ improves/controls Openplace service and manages Openplace contents' lifecycle.

- Management of Knowledge Contents. Plans and operates knowledge contents and carries out related improvement activities and manages knowledge according to its lifecycle … so that it can be created and utilized.

- Management of Knowledge Assets. Manages knowledge assetization activities by establishing principles and standards about onsite KM activities, maintains/manages the quality of acquired knowledge assets, and operates knowledge services so that employees can utilize and reuse knowledge.

- Management of Knowledge Network. In order to operate knowledge assets effectively, manages collaboration activities with KM experts and their resumes and operates and manages research clubs/communities and cyber consulting.

- Management of KM Organization Culture. Plans and operates change management issues required in pursuing KM innovation activities and communication programs.

- Management of KM Activity Results. Defines KPI for results of KM activities and measure/monitors/analyzes/evaluates/compensates by defining performance and standards for KM.

- Key skills. Must be aware of an organization's roles and responsibilities and must have an understanding of each organization's business execution. Must have an extensive understanding and experiences in all corporate activities, must define knowledge required to execute an enterprise's job functions in each area and each business, and must have an ability to develop and execute a strategy required to acquire/use knowledge.

- Career plan. A Knowledge Manager can grow into a KM consultant and can become a Chief Knowledge Officer based on such expertise.

This is a fairly typical role description for a strategic level knowledge manager. The only thing we would add to this description is that the knowledge manager does not only develop the strategy, but also works with management to implement it. There are many elements to this job description which are specific to Samsung, which represent parts of the management framework they have introduced for KM; for example Networks, Knowledge Assets, and Openplace (Samsung's online portal).

Other Roles in KM

Besides the role of knowledge manager there are several other individual and group roles that are critical to the success of a KM Program. The specific role names may change to meet the needs of your organization's culture; it is the underlying activities and responsibilities that are critical. These roles may not yet be in place in your organization, and part of your strategy work, and part of the development of the KM framework, is to define which roles you will need to introduce.

KM Team

You will almost certainly need a KM team to help you deliver the strategy, the team will be cross-functional, and cross-organizational in order to maintain KM's relevance and alignment to the organization. The KM team is described in detail in Chapter 19.

KM Sponsor

It is the responsibility of the KM sponsor to:

- Act as customer for the KM strategy

- Agree to (or reject) the strategy

- Provide resources for implementation of the strategy

- Act as champion for KM within the organization

- Aid in removal of any roadblocks to implementation of the strategy

Steering Team

The sponsor often appoints a high-level steering team or committee to provide guidance for KM implementation, and to act as a "coalition for change." The role of the steering team/committee is discussed in detail in Chapter 19.

Roles within the KM Framework

There will be a number of specific roles which you will introduce within the KM framework. These are introduced in Chapter 13, and might include some of the following;

- Community of Practice leader

- Community facilitator

- Community sponsor

- Roles to support knowledge capture, for example facilitators, learning historians, project knowledge managers

- Knowledge owners

- Subject matter experts

- Lessons management team

In addition, everyone in the organization has a part to play in KM, even if they don't hold a specific KM role. Their part is to seek out knowledge from others, and share new knowledge with those who need it.

Summary and Next Steps

Understanding your own role is crucial. You need to ensure your role covers the four key elements, with more detail included where needed.

You also need to be aware of the other roles that will be needed within KM; both the roles involved with KM implementation, and roles within the KM framework. Once you are clear on the roles, then it is time to move on to the next step—making a case to senior management for crafting a KM strategy.

Note

1.   "What is Knowledge Management?" http://www.sds.samsung.com/career/work/job/knowledge_manage.jsp. Accessed May 27, 2014.

CHAPTER 3

Making the Case for a Knowledge Management Strategy

Before you can consider drafting a Knowledge Management (KM) strategy, you may need to make a more general case for KM, and for actually having a strategy in the first place. Creation of a strategy is a small project in itself, and in order to embark on this work you may have to make a case to management that:

a) Knowledge is an asset for your organization

b) Knowledge is currently being managed sub-optimally, and

c) The organization needs a KM strategy

Is Knowledge a Key Business Issue for You?

If knowledge is a key business driver in your organization, or if knowledge is one of your key products, then KM is likely to be important for you. Knowledge is defined by Peter Senge[1] as "the ability to take effective action," and knowledge is the basis both of judgment and of good decision making; so to the extent that you need to make knowledgeable decisions as part of good business practice, knowledge is an asset for your business. This principle is expanded further in the following list:

- If your organization requires good knowledge-based decisions, then knowledge is one of your key assets

- If you are a consulting firm, a contractor, or an educational or professional body that creates and deploys knowledge on behalf of customers and clients, then again knowledge is one of your key assets

- When crucial knowledge is at risk through retirement or redundancy of key staff, then retaining that knowledge is a significant business issue

- Where you are involved in repeat activity, then transfer of knowledge from the past to help improve future performance can be an important component of continuous cost reduction or quality improvement

- If dispersed parts of the business are performing the same process with varying results, this is evidence that some parts of the business know how to perform operations better than other parts, and that knowledge needs to be shared and reused

- Knowledge is a key business issue for you if your budget is being challenged and you have to contemplate delivering "more for less," or, to use a business cliché, "working smarter, not harder." Working smarter means making better use of your organizational knowledge

Is There Evidence That Management of Knowledge Might Be Sub-Optimal in Your Organization?

There may be many warning signs that KM needs to be improved in an organization. If you keep hearing any of the statements that follow, then the management of knowledge is not working well.

- 'Why do we keep having to relearn this?'

- 'How do I know where to find this knowledge?'

- 'I'm sure I heard someone mention that to me the other day, now who was it?'

- 'Someone must have done this before—but who?'

- 'When that guy left, he took all that knowledge with him'

- 'It was pure luck that I met Freddy/Susie—he/she had just the answer I was looking for'

- 'That went very well—how do we repeat that success?'

- 'We made this mistake in our other office too'

Comments like this are all warning signs. Others include:

- Repeated mistakes

- Wildly varying performance among different teams

- Poorly connected networks (see Figure 3.1)

You need to collect evidence, in the form of anecdotes, examples, and social network plots such as the ones previously mentioned, which show that KM could be improved.

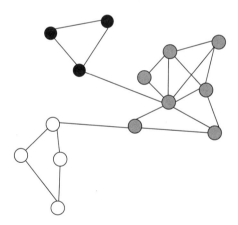

Figure 3.1   A poorly connected network

Is It Likely That Improved KM Might Add Real Value?

If you do improve KM, is it likely that this would lead to better performance? Better performance could come through eliminated mistakes, from more consistent performance (with poor performing teams learning from high performing teams), from faster transfer of knowledge to young staff, and from better retention of knowledge from departing staff.

You need to be able to make a good case that there is potential value here; enough value to investigate KM further. You are not making a full business case for KM implementation; this business case will be made in the next stage. You are, however, marshalling the anecdotal evidence that performance improvement is possible, and that this is potentially significant enough to take the next step of investigating KM further.

What Evidence Do You Need to Collect?

To make the case for further investment, it is good to have the following evidence:

- A first-pass list of critical knowledge issues for the organization

- Evidence, in the form of examples, case studies, anecdotes, Social Network Maps or other evidence, that there is a KM problem, and

- A list of likely positive business outcomes from better KM

Who Makes the Decision to Invest?

You are marshalling the evidence to allow an investment decision; the investment in further investigation of KM. This investigation may potentially include an assessment of current KM capability, and certainly will include the development of a KM strategy and implementation plan. Therefore, the person making the decision has to have budgetary authority for taking these steps and commissioning these actions. They also need to be senior enough in the organization that they can influence the decision that comes after the assessment program, which is the piloting decision. They don't need to be a C-level executive, but could be a regional manager, the head of a division, or a senior manager of similar status.

However, you are going to need input from the C-level executives in order to craft your strategy. Therefore, it makes sense for these high-level people to be involved in the decision to invest in further investigation.

What Exactly Are You Asking Them to Decide?

The decision you are asking for is to commission a further investigation of KM, ideally including a current state assessment, potentially including a scan of existing knowledge topics, and definitely including development of a KM strategy, in order to see exactly what needs to be done to bring KM up to the required level of quality.

Basically, you are asking them to fund the development of your strategy.

Summary and Next Steps

Making the case to senior managers for investment in KM is an important step. If you can show that knowledge is an important business driver, that the firm's current management of knowledge is sub-optimal, and that KM will turn this around, then you should be able to make a credible case for investigating KM. Once you have this investment promise, it's time to start thinking about the principles behind the KM strategy itself.

Note

1.   Peter Senge, Keynote speech at the KM Asia Conference, 2004.

The Ten Principles Behind Your KM Strategy

Knowledge Management (KM) has been around nearly two decades now with as many failures as successes. What usually separates the successes from the failures are the principles behind each of the programs. KM programs based on sound principles succeed; those that are not fail. In this chapter we list 10 key strategic principles for KM, and then expand on each of them.

Your KM strategy should be based on these principles, so you'll want to discuss them with your steering team, gain consensus on basing your KM program on them, and document them in the strategy. The rest of your strategy depends on your adopting these principles.

This is a long chapter, reflecting its importance. Get the principles right and success will follow.

KM Strategic Principles

1. KM implementation needs to be organization-led; tied to organization strategy and to specific organization issues

2. KM needs to be delivered where the critical knowledge lies, and where the high value decisions are made

3. KM implementation needs to be treated as a behavior change program

4. The endgame will be to introduce a complete management framework for KM

5. This framework will need to be embedded into the organization structures

6. The framework will need to include governance if it is to be sustainable

7. The framework will be structured, rather than emergent

8. A KM implementation should be a staged process, with regular decision points

9. A KM implementation should contain a piloting stage

10. A KM implementation should be run by an implementation team, reporting to a cross-organizational steering group

Now let's look at these 10 principles one by one.

1. KM Implementation Needs to Be Organization-Led

Black & Decker used to say "Our customers don't want a power drill; they want holes in the wall."

Similarly in KM, the senior managers don't want "a KM system," they don't want "Enterprise 2.0," and they don't want "more knowledge sharing"—they want a Better Organization (better decisions, better practices, and fewer repeat mistakes). They want to make sure that decision-making staff at all levels in the organization have access to the knowledge they need to help them to make the best decisions and deliver the best results. It's up to you, the knowledge manager, to develop and implement the strategy that will make it happen.

Neither do organization staff "want KM"; what they want is an easier way to find the knowledge they need to solve their problems, and a wider stage on which to use their own knowledge. Again, it's up to you, the knowledge manager, to develop and implement the KM framework that will make it happen.

If we are going to do our jobs properly as knowledge managers, we need to start from organizational strategy, organizational needs, and organizational outcomes at all levels. It is vital that KM efforts are linked to organizational outcomes, because the outcomes are what are important. This principle has been recognized by many of the early writers in the knowledge management field, and there are plenty of stories to support this as being the only effective approach. Consider, for instance:

- This quote from an early '00s survey: "Most successful KM applications addressed a 'life or death' business situation. Successful cases answered two questions at the outset: What business objective am I trying to achieve? How can I apply existing knowledge?"[1]

- This quote attributed to Bechtel Corporation in the late '90s: "KM is not an end in itself. Companies do not exist for the purpose of propagating and advancing knowledge—they exist to sell products and services. But to the extent that competitive advantage relies on informed decision-making within the business, KM has a crucial role to play."

- Tom Davenport and co-authors, in the paper "Building Successful KM Projects"[2] conclude that "Link to economic performance or industry value" is the number one success factor for KM.

- The head of IT at BP recognized this when he said, "We have been looking at the key processes of the business, testing them for their knowledge intensity to see if we would create some significant new change in the performance of that particular process if we managed knowledge in a more profound way. This concept has not been difficult to sell to the top executive team."[3]

The story is told of how President John F. Kennedy, on a visit to NASA, encountered a janitor and asked him what his job was. The janitor replied, "To help to put a man on the moon." There is some discussion of whether or not the story is true, but what it illustrates is the janitor's complete alignment with the aims of NASA, and the collective mission and strategy of the organization.

What if it had been the KM lead at NASA whom Kennedy had spoken to? What sort of answer would he have received? Hopefully the KM program was also strategic, and also linked to the collective mission and strategy of the organization. However, a lot of KM professionals haven't made this link. If you ask them what they are doing, they'll say "We're rolling out SharePoint," or, "I am trialing MediaWiki." This would be the equivalent of the NASA janitor saying "I'm trying out a new mop head." The link from the organizational priorities to the KM effort has been lost.

2. KM Needs to Be Delivered Where the Critical Knowledge Lies, and Where the High Value Decisions Are Made

We suggest that one of the first questions the KM professional needs to ask management is "*What knowledge?*"

What knowledge is important? What knowledge needs to be managed? What knowledge should be the focus of your KM activity? You don't have to manage *all* of the knowledge; only in those areas which truly add business value; the "critical knowledge areas." This critical knowledge will be knowledge that is crucial to the strategy of the organization, and which therefore needs to drive your KM strategy. The senior managers of the organization will help you determine what these knowledge areas are, and the first bullet point list in Chapter 3 will give you guidance on where critical knowledge lies.

Often our default approach as knowledge managers is to think that this critical knowledge is technical knowledge held by people at lower levels in the organization; the "knowledge workers" such as the sales force, the plant operators or the project engineers. However, this viewpoint misses the significant value and opportunity of applying KM at a middle and senior management level. Middle managers and senior managers are knowledge workers too, and there is as much value from influencing the relatively rare but very high value decisions that project managers, divisional managers and senior managers make as there is in supporting the much more common but much lower value decisions of the front line staff.

One of the most valuable pieces of work done at BP, for example, was at senior management level, taking the knowledge and lessons from the Amoco merger and applying them to the Arco acquisition. There we were working with the CFO, the chief counsel, and one of the VPs; very senior level people whose knowledge and experience from the Amoco merger really accelerated the Arco process, and made for a much smoother transition to an integrated organization.

Delivering a high-level KM pilot at a senior level has three benefits:

- It delivers significant value to the organization

- It engages senior managers in KM, and helps them understand the value KM can bring to the organization as a whole

- It gains senior managers' buy-in, by showing how KM can solve their most pressing problems

KM is something that is needed at all levels, and the sooner you involve the senior managers, the faster and smoother your implementation will become. So make sure your critical knowledge areas include the big topics such as mergers, acquisitions, divestments, integrations, new market entry, organization restructuring, and recession survival. Not only do you deliver huge value, you may well get instant buy-in from the very people you most need on your side.

3. KM Implementation Should Be Treated as a Behavior Change Management Exercise

KM is a program that implements and manages organizational change and should be treated as such. It is not about buying and rolling out technology, it is not about giving people new toys, and it is not about adding another task into the project framework—it is about changing the way people think. It is about changing personal and organizational priorities, and it is about changing the way people treat knowledge. It is a profound shift from the individual to the social collective, involving the following changes in emphasis:

- From "I know" to "We know"

- From "Knowledge is mine" to "Knowledge is ours"

- From "Knowledge is owned" to "Knowledge is shared"

- From "Knowledge is personal property" to "Knowledge is collective/community property"

- From "Knowledge is personal advantage" to "Knowledge is company advantage"

- From "Knowledge is personal" to "Knowledge is inter-personal"

- From "I defend what I know" to "I am open to better knowledge"

- From "Not invented here (i.e., by me)" to "Invented in my community"

- From "New knowledge competes with my personal knowledge" to "New knowledge improves my personal knowledge"

- From "Other people's knowledge is a threat to me" to "Our shared knowledge helps me"

- From "Admitting that I don't know is a weakness" to "Admitting that I don't know is the first step to learning"

KM should be introduced as an organizational change program, with high-level sponsorship, with a communication strategy, with a desired result, and with phased implementation rather than "everyone change at once." Change follows the S-curve, change has to reach a tipping point, and hearts and minds are changed one at a time. Organizational change is a well-established discipline, and KM needs to incorporate this discipline in its execution.

The change in emphasis and behavior we are talking about here is not a gradual change; it is a step-change. It is a remodeling of the organization; a makeover, and a new way of thinking. It needs to be treated as a change process and measured as a change process. Don't go into KM thinking that it is about a new IT tool, or trying out communities of practice —you won't get far if you don't start to address hearts and minds and behaviors. This means that KM implementation must be structured using change management principles, including a piloting component, and must have a strong team of change agents to implement the change.

4. The Endgame Will Be to Introduce a Complete Management Framework for KM

The ultimate goal of your Knowledge Management strategy will be to introduce a KM framework into the working processes of the organization. Nancy Dixon has posted some very interesting ideas about the evolution of KM, and how it has evolved from Information and Content Management, to Networking and Experiential Knowledge, to Collective

Organizational Knowledge[4]. Similarly we have seen an evolution in the understanding of just what is needed in terms of a complete management framework for KM. We can look at this evolution by briefly reviewing the KM history of one of the authors of *Designing a Successful KM Strategy*.

Evolutionary Stage 1—Focus on One or Two Tools

When author Nick Milton was working in Norway in the early to mid-'90s, his KM approach was very simple, focusing on one or two KM components: the retrospect, and a lessons database. In hindsight this was a naive and rudimentary approach, and the lessons built up in the database until it became too full and too daunting for people to use as reference. He was focusing on one or two tools, and missing large chunks of KM.

There are quite a few organizations still at this stage. They have bought an Enterprise Content Management system or a social networking platform, or are capturing lessons, and think that this alone will deliver KM. But no one tool alone will deliver KM.

Evolutionary Stage 2—Build a Toolbox

When Nick left Norway in 1997 and joined the BP KM team, the team had already realized they needed more than one KM tool. This is when Nick and colleagues developed the "learning before, during, and after" model, and started to put together a KM toolbox including "after-action reviews," "peer assist," and the concept of "knowledge assets." Certainly that gave a little more in the way of success, but the success was largely down to the intervention of the KM team, and when the KM team withdrew, knowledge-sharing died away. That's because a toolbox is not enough. The BP toolbox was not embedded into the work practices of the organization, the roles were not in place, and there was no governance. The attitude the KM team was taking was "Here are a bunch of tools—we invite you to use them to deliver value." And, largely, the organization declined the invitation.

There are many organizations at this stage. They have defined a KM toolbox—in some cases an extensive toolbox, and sometimes a very expensive one as well. But KM remains optional, and it remains separate from the everyday work process. A toolbox alone will not deliver sustainable KM.

Evolutionary Stage 3—Implement a Framework

When Nick left BP in 1999, KM was still at the toolbox stage. In 2004 Nick and his colleague Tom Young worked with BP again to do a major review of KM, and to look at where it was working, and what was missing. That's where the concept was born of a "KM framework"—a set of KM activities embedded into organization process, a number of roles embedded into the organizational structure, and a selection of supporting technologies, all under an umbrella of governance.[5] At last, KM was beginning to take on the aspects of other management systems, as a framework of roles, processes, technologies, and governance, which could be made part of the organization.

Where KM works well—in the military, for example—there is always such a framework in place. Any successful KM implementation needs to look beyond single tools or toolboxes, and aim to implement a management framework of processes, roles, technologies, and governance.

5. The Framework Must Be Embedded Into the Organization Structures

If your KM framework is not embedded into the existing organizational structures, you risk reverting to a pre-KM state later on. Many of the high-profile, late-stage failures of KM are due to a failure to embed.

Stephen Denning has published an interesting and thought-provoking post, entitled "Why Do Great KM Programs Fail?"[6] where he concludes that, "Even when an oasis of excellence and innovation is established within an organization being run on traditional management lines, the experience doesn't take root and replicate throughout the organization."

Late-stage failures such as those described by Denning often occur because KM has not been embedded in normal organizational activities. These programs are often delivered by a strong team and a charismatic leader, but delivered as something separate, and not fully rooted in the work structure and management framework of the organization.

For KM to succeed in the long term, the processes, roles, technology, and governance must be incorporated into day-to-day structures such as the project management system, the quality management system, and the sales process.

6. The Framework Will Need to Include Governance If It Is to Be Sustainable

Without governance, embedding a framework for KM in the operations of the organization will not result in lasting and sustained change to KM behaviors and culture. Governance in this case refers to the on-going organizational elements that must be in place to ensure that an asset—in this case knowledge—is managed properly and with rigor in a sustained way.

If you are a manager and you want to get something done in your organization, you need to set three things in place:

- First, you have to make it very clear what you want done

- Second, you have to give people the tools and the training to do it

- Third, you have to check that they've done what you asked them to

These three elements are important governance components in all areas of life. If you wanted to get your teenage son or daughter to mow the lawn, for example, you would first be very clear with them about what you expected them to do; next, you would show them where the lawnmower is and explain how to use it; and, finally, you would check that they had completed the work.

Without the clarity of expectation and explanation, your son or daughter would most likely claim that they weren't sure what to do, or else they would do only half the job, leaving the edges untrimmed and the grass clippings all over the lawn. If you didn't give them the lawnmower and show them how to use it, they wouldn't be able to get started. If you didn't check up on them, the likelihood is that they would be distracted by more urgent activities such as the PlayStation,

Twitter, or Facebook. Those three elements—clarity of expectation, the tools to do the job, and monitoring—ensure the job gets done. It's a governance system for mowing the lawn!

Your strategy must ensure that a similar governance framework is applied to KM. Imagine if the staff in your organization knew that they had to do a knowledge budget (or other learning and planning activity) at the start of any significant piece of work. Imagine they knew that they would have to do knowledge tracking as the work continues, and balance the knowledge books by capturing their learning at the end of the job. Imagine that they had the tools to do these activities, and the training to use the tools, and also that management would be checking to see that they had done what they were supposed to do. Whether or not the individual employee believes KM is a good thing, such a governance system will ensure that it happens.

7. The Framework Will Be Structured, Rather Than Emergent

There is a major philosophical divide in KM circles between the Structured and the Emergent camps.

The Emergent people believe that if you provide people with the tools, then knowledge sharing will naturally emerge. They point to Wikipedia as a prime example of this—the wisdom of the crowds spontaneously emerging as documented knowledge. They point to Twitter, to LinkedIn, and to many other global social networking tools. They believe that knowledge is organic, and that too much management will kill it. This was the prevalent view a decade ago, particularly where communities of practice were concerned.

The Structured people believe that knowledge is an asset to an organization, and that assets cannot safely be left to manage themselves. They believe that if there is an area of knowledge which is important to the organization, then there should be a community of practice that looks after that knowledge. Rather than waiting for such a community of practice to spontaneously emerge, they encourage it.

ConocoPhillips is a prime example of the structured knowledge company: they divide their business into areas of competence, and for each area they ensure there is a community of practice and a network leader, who is also the editor of the relevant wiki page. The network leaders are given training, and the communities are nurtured through a growth process until they become highly effective knowledge-sharing mechanisms. Each network leader reports upward through functional excellence teams into the functional leadership of the organization.

The past 10 years has seen a shift, with the Structured view becoming dominant, at least for KM within organizations, and the Emergent view less dominant. This change has come through experience with working with knowledge sharing within organizations, and the need to adapt and structure the corporate intranet free-for-all, which was modeled on the internet, into a managed system with an architecture that allows staff to find and use the knowledge they need to get their jobs done efficiently and effectively.

Unstructured networking similar to that seen on the internet is not a useful model for knowledge sharing in organizations, for these reasons:

- The emergent discussion forums in LinkedIn very quickly fragment into multiple parallel conversations, which often deteriorate further into silos. That is a disaster in an organization where there needs to be one place to go to tap into a network, not 422 places.

- The 90:9:1 participation model of Wikipedia is fine if there is a massive pool of potential contributors, with redundancy in knowledge. Tapping into what is effectively 2 or 3 percent of the available knowledge is fine, if the available knowledge is global. In an organization, it just isn't enough.

- The diversity profile of Wikipedia is highly skewed. If your organization knowledge base was disproportionally populated by the knowledge of unmarried males under the age of 30, as Wikipedia is, you would think something was amiss.

The prevalent Emergent view of KM a decade ago derived from an assessment that knowledge is organic, and that it could be killed by too much control. However, structure does not necessarily require control, and structure can be applied to the management of organic things.

The classical structured organic enterprise is the garden—the flower garden, the vegetable garden, the market garden, the allotment.

The vegetables grow organically, within a structure. And anyone with a garden will know that if you want to produce flowers or vegetables, then "organic" is hard work, and requires a lot of management. You don't just "let the garden emerge," because all you'll get is weeds. If you simply 'let a thousand flowers bloom" most of them will be dandelions; few if any will be tomato plants. Instead, you create the conditions, fertilize the soil, plant the seeds, remove the weeds, deter the pests, tend and water and fertilize, and eventually your flowers and vegetables will grow. If knowledge is organic, then KM is akin to gardening, with all the structure that this implies.

Your strategy should be a structured one, rather than an emergent one. Find out what knowledge is critical to the success of the organization, and put in place the framework and structure that ensures it will be managed.

8. A KM Implementation Should Be a Staged Process, With Regular Decision Points

Implementing KM into an organization will not happen accidentally. It happens by making a deliberate decision, or rather a series of decisions, each one followed by much hard work until the next review/decision point.

Very few company presidents or CEOs wake up one morning and "decide" to implement KM. Instead, like any other practice, implementation will follow a series of decisions, with each decision resting on a basis of necessary evidence.

The decision chain is shown in Figure 4.1 and in the five decisions that follow.

Decision 1: To Investigate KM

Your first decision will be to set up a task force to determine whether or not KM makes operational sense for the organization. The task force will study the pros and cons and decide if it is worthwhile pursuing. Assuming an affirmative decision, the task force will then make the business case for investing in KM.

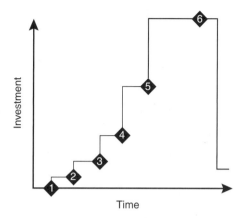

Figure 4.1   Stepwise investment in Knowledge Management implementation

Decision 2: To Map Out What Needs to Be Done to Implement KM

If the task force has shown that KM makes good operational sense, then further work is needed to assess the current state, to define the KM strategy and implementation plan, and to estimate the time, budget, and resources required. We are assuming that this is the stage you have already reached; the stage at which you need *Designing a Successful KM Strategy.*

Decision 3: To Pilot KM in High-Profile Areas

If the strategy, plan and budget are approved, then KM needs to be piloted in selected business areas in order to road-test and refine the KM framework prior to roll-out. By this time, KM is becoming quite high profile, and quite high cost.

Decision 4: To Roll Out KM as a Required Discipline to the Whole Organization

If the pilots were successful and the value of KM to the organization and to the employees was proven, the next decision—not to be taken lightly!—is to roll out a KM framework across the whole organization. This is the point of no return.

Decision 5: To Stand Down the Implementation Team

After the KM program has been rolled out across the organization, it's time to hand over KM to be managed as part of normal operational processes and disband the implementation team. The KM team must be sure that KM is fully embedded before making this decision.

Treating KM as a series of incremental decisions as just described has two main benefits. First, it is sensible, prudent decision-making. Figure 4.1 shows that the investment in each stage will be a little larger than the previous stage—a task force costs less than a team, which costs less than a series of pilots, which costs less than a roll-out campaign. Each incremental increase in cost is built on a decision, which depends on the results of the previous stage, and on how well KM has proven itself. And at any point up until Decision 4, the organization can change its mind, because it is not fully committed. Once Decision 4 is taken, the organization is committed to roll-out.

And that's the second advantage. If each decision is made by the right people, based on the right information and the right criteria, then you shouldn't have to revisit the decisions later. Each decision should be documented, and should stand on its own merits. You shouldn't have to keep re-justifying, and remaking decisions. Decision 5—the decision to roll out KM—needs to be made at the highest level. You need the support of the CEO to make an organization-wide change like this. But by the time it comes to Decision 4, a series of successful trials and pilots will have demonstrated that KM works in your organization, and delivers real value.

9. A KM Implementation Should Contain a Piloting Stage

In generic terms, there are three main implementation strategies for KM, and only one of them is, in our experience, really reliable. These are shown symbolically in Figure 4.2.

You ultimately want all the elements of the KM framework deployed across all of the organization. You want to get to the grey square in the top right of Figure 4.2, marked with the number 4.

There are three ways to get there:

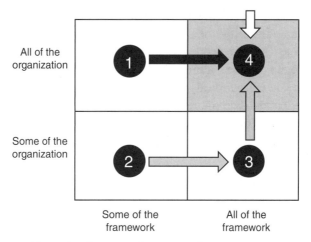

Figure 4.2   Three implementation strategies

1. The white arrow represents getting there in one step—planning a framework, and then rolling it out across the whole organization. This is a high risk strategy. You only get one shot at the framework design, and if you get it wrong, it may be permanently wrong. Also you will be beginning the roll-out with no history of success within the organization, which makes change management difficult (as explained in Chapter 13).

2. The black arrow represents rolling out parts of the framework one by one across the whole organization (Circle 1) until the framework is complete. This is a common approach, and people often start by rolling out the technology element, and only later introducing the other elements of roles and accountabilities, processes and governance. This also is a high risk strategy. Few framework elements add much value when working in isolation, and you may devalue the whole KM implementation if you introduce something that adds no value. Often people will roll out a technology such as Groupware, social media, or enterprise search, and find that knowledge sharing and reuse do not automatically follow. By which time, you may have devalued KM as a concept, and you may not get a second chance.

3. The grey arrow represents a piloted implementation. At Circle 2, you test elements of the framework one by one, locally in the

organization, to make sure they work in the organization context, and to tailor them until they do. At Circle 3, you pilot the whole KM framework in one part of the organization, to make sure the complete framework adds value to the organization, and you tailor it until it does. Finally (Circle 4) you roll out this tried, tested, and piloted framework across the organization as a whole. The piloting strategy represented by the grey arrow takes longer, but it has a much higher chance of success.

In the third approach, the pilot is a crucial element, and is a test of Knowledge Management as a whole, rather than one or two KM tools in isolation. Piloting is, therefore, a large-scale test of KM and a prototype of the KM framework.

In the late 1990s we worked with Colonel Ed Guthrie of the U.S. Army, whose view of KM was similar to this model. His model was based on how you might get a brigade across a river. You start with firing a rope over the river, use the rope to pull across a pontoon bridge, and march the rest of the army over the bridge. In his model the far bank of the river is the changed KM behavior, with KM embedded and applied, and the early KM pilots are the rope.

The other advantage of piloting over an "everything at once" implementation is that it delivers some quick wins to management. When the CEO comes by and asks, "How are we progressing with KM?" it's great to be able to say "We've been working with X division and Y community and we've got some really good success stories to tell you." Additionally, you can use these pilot-based success stories as internal marketing material to help with the behavior change element of roll-out.

10. A KM Implementation Should Be Run as a Project

During the implementation stage, KM is a project, one that is set up to implement change in the organization, and to move the organization to a state where KM is embedded as part of the way the organization operates. As with any project, there are a number of roles and accountabilities associated with delivering the project objectives. These include:

- KM project leader or Chief Knowledge Officer

- KM implementation team

- KM project sponsor

- Management steering team

In addition to these roles, your KM implementation project will need a budget, an implementation plan, and a set of milestones and objectives. The end point of the project will be a fully implemented and embedded KM framework—in place, delivering value, with governance in place, and sustainable.

Example of Principles Within a KM Strategy

Given that the principles behind any strategy are important, and should be made explicit, it is surprising that relatively few published KM strategies make reference to principles. An exception is the KM strategy for the STAR (Strengthening Transparency and Responsiveness) program in Ghana,[7] a multi-donor-pooled funding mechanism (funded by DFID, DANIDA, EU, and USAID) to increase the influence of civil society and Parliament in the governance of public goods and service delivery, with the ultimate goal of improving the accountability and responsiveness of Ghana's government, traditional authorities, and the private sector.

The STAR-Ghana KM strategy outlines a set of nine principles, which follow. Some of these read more like vision statements than principles, per se (number 5, for instance), but others mirror the principles covered in this chapter. The first principle on the STAR-Ghana list matches our number one principle, which is the most important of all the KM principles we've discussed.

[STAR-Ghana's] core KM guiding principles are as follows:

- The KM strategy must be aligned to the shared vision and values of STAR-Ghana

- STAR-Ghana and grantees are 'learning organizations' and are encouraged to be innovative and try out new approaches and initiatives in KM

- Work processes and systems must be improved to include more collective, systematic and continuous learning and knowledge processes

- We need to allocate time and budget to KM

- Every time we do something repetitive we should strive to do it better than the last time

- Knowledge systems and tools developed encourage ownership of the institutional and intellectual memories of the organization. They should be to support knowledge asset driven strategies, processes, methods and techniques

- Grant Partners, stakeholders and the citizen need to have access to information generated about and from our work and has to be timely

- STAR-Ghana KM is concerned with creating, sharing and applying knowledge as a team, by working more effectively together as one. Communicate, learn and share knowledge

- Leverage knowledge for achieving organizational goals and serving citizens and noncitizens

Summary and Next Steps

An effective KM strategy will rest on proven principles. The ten principles described in this chapter are the foundation of your KM strategy and program. They have been identified out of the experience of the authors and are generally acknowledged as best practices across the field of KM, regardless of industry or sector. Once you are clear on the principles, it's time to move on to the next step: creating your strategy document.

Notes

1. Teltech survey, source now lost.
2. Thomas H. Davenport, David W. De Long, and Michael C. Beers, "Building Successful KM Projects," in *Managing the Knowledge of the Organization* (Ernst & Young LLP, 1997). http://www.providersedge.com/docs/km_articles/Building_Successful_KM_Projects.pdf
3. John Cross, BP CIO, interviewed in CIO Magazine, May 5, 1997, 120.

4. Nancy Dixon, "Where Knowledge Management Has Been and Where It Is Going-Part Three," July 30, 2009, accessed May 27, 2014, www.nancydixonblog.com/2009/07/where-knowledge-management-has-been-and-where-it-is-going-part-three.html.

5. P. J. Gibby, N. Milton, W. A. Palen, and S. E. Hensley, *Implementing a Framework for KM*. SPE-101315-PP: (Society of Petroleum Engineers, 2006).

6. Steve Denning, "Why Do Great KM Programs Fail?" *The Leader's Guide to Radical Management*, July 4, 2010, accessed Jan. 2014, stevedenning.typepad.com/steve_denning/2010/07/why-do-great-km-programs-fail.html.

7. STAR-Ghana, "KNOWLEDGE MANAGEMENT STRATEGY - May 2011," accessed May 27, 2014, http://www.starghana.org/userfiles/files/publications/KM%20STRATEGY.pdf.

CHAPTER 5

Strategy Structure, and Strategy Input

Once you have discussed and agreed on a set of guiding principles, it's time to start creating your Knowledge Management (KM) strategy document. To begin, your outline should include these 11 sections:

1. Strategic KM principles

2. The organizational imperative and focus for KM

3. A KM vision for the organization

4. Critical knowledge areas

5. Stakeholders

6. A KM framework

7. Information management

8. Change management

9. Business case

10. Recommended pilots

11. Next steps

You can write Section 1 yourself, and we recommend that you base it on the strategic principles we gave you in Chapter 2. These are tried and tested principles, based on sound experience, and should apply to every organization. Sections 6 and 7—KM framework and information management—are two of the other sections you can write yourself. Sections on change management and the business case can also be undertaken with limited senior input.

The rest of the sections will require significant input from within your organization, especially from the managers. You can't write an effective strategy without extensive input from others. You can either collect the input through a series of interviews and summarize it yourself, or you can hold a series of workshops to capture, discuss, summarize, and validate the input. Whether you do it through interviews or workshops, you will need to speak to the following people:

- The heads of the operational units within the organization

- The heads of any functional units (the head of engineering, head of marketing, head of sales, etc.)

- The heads of the relevant support organizations, particularly the head of information technology and the head of human resources

As we discuss the various sections of the strategy within the chapters of *Designing a Successful KM Strategy* that follow, we will recommend approaches you can apply to create the contents of your strategy document, using either interviews or workshops to gather input. Here, we'll look at these two approaches in a little more detail.

Interview Approach

With the interview approach, you need to make a list of the senior people whose input you need, and then ask each of them to spend an hour or two with you. During the course of your interviews you need to find out:

- Their vision for KM

- Where they think KM can most help the organization

- What knowledge they view as being of the greatest value to the organization

- Who they think the key stakeholders are who need to be engaged with KM implementation.

- Where they think the best potential pilot areas are for KM implementation

You will then need to collate everyone's input, compile it, and feed it back to them at a later date either as a strategy document, or, even better, during a strategy feedback and validation workshop.

Workshop Approach

If you can get commitment from your senior people to invest a significant amount of time in a KM strategy creation workshop, then you have the opportunity to create and compile participants' input at the same time. This allows for a greater breadth and depth of discussion on the scope of the KM strategy.

The length of time needed for the workshop depends on the size of the organization, the scale of the program, and the amount of buy-in you are trying to generate. Three examples of workshop agendas follow; the first was from a small organization where we had done a fair amount of pre-work, the second is from a three-day strategy workshop run by Nancy Dixon for Ecopetrol, the Colombian State petroleum company (described on Nancy's blog[1]), and the third is a session held to build a KM strategy for a single business unit.

Example One-Day Workshop for a Small Organization

Attendees:

- Head of Division
- Head of Division
- IT Director
- Research & Development Director
- Operations Director
- Head of Planning
- Head of Business Development

Example Two-And-A-Half-Day Workshop, as Run at Ecopetrol

Attendees:

- Company president
- Top 200 people in the organization

Table 5.1 Strategy workshop for a small organization

Time	Module	Purpose
10:00	Introduction, models, definitions, case histories	A shared discussion on Knowledge Management, to get clarity on the ideas and options, and develop a shared understanding of KM models for the organization.
11:30	Key knowledge areas	An understanding of the knowledge areas which most need to be managed to enable the organization to meet its goals.
12:30	Lunch	
1:00	Business benefits	Looking at the possible KM interventions, and mapping out how they can add value to the business.
2:30	Stakeholder analysis	Looking at the issues of implementing KM, deciding who the key stakeholder groupings might be, and developing a view of how and when they will need to be engaged.
4:00	Pilot options	Brainstorm of areas within the organization where KM may deliver quick wins.
4:30	Finish	

- External experts (in this case, Nancy Dixon and Larry Prusak)
- Representatives from external organizations

Example of a Departmental or Business Unit Workshop

Rather than an organization-wide KM strategy you may be tasked with creating a KM strategy for your department or business unit. If this is the case, the workshops and interviews cover the same material but you may have a different level of participation in the strategy development process. You may interview senior management individually and hold workshops for front-line managers and employees. In this case your workshop agenda may resemble that in Table 5.3.

Table 5.2   Strategy agenda for a large organization as described by Nancy Dixon[1]

Component	Module	Purpose
Day one	Knowledge management principles	15-minute presentations from experts and external organizations, followed by small group conversations (to input ideas and experience from others into the room).
Day two morning	Critical knowledge areas	Multiple knowledge cafés to address the question "what knowledge do we need at Ecopetrol that we don't have."
Day two afternoon	Potential pilots and other actions	Open space technology, building on the outputs from the knowledge cafés, to identify improvement actions and pilots to make knowledge management a reality.
Day three morning	Summary and action plan	Summary of the conversations, inputs and conclusions from the previous two days.

Table 5.3   Strategy meeting agenda for a department

Time	Module	Content
30 minutes	Introduction	• Review knowledge management concepts • Review project motivation
2 hours	Questions and discussion	• Strategic objectives • Process and activities to be enabled with knowledge management • Information flows • Use of knowledge • Knowledge lifecycle activities
10 minutes	Next steps	

The three examples shown in the table will give you some idea of the "ends of the scale" when it comes to KM strategy creation workshops. You will need to choose a solution that fits the scale of your organization and the number of people who need to attend.

Summary and Next Steps

By now you will have an idea not only of the structure of your KM strategy document, but also of the methods you will use to gather the data needed to write each of the main sections. The first section we will start work on is the section on the organizational imperatives and drivers.

Note

1. Nancy Dixon, "A KM Strategy Built on the Collective Knowledge of Ecopetrol," Conversation Matters blog, July 04, 2009, accessed May 27, 2014, www.nancydixonblog.com/2009/07/a-km-strategy-built-on-the-collective-knowledge-of-ecopetrol.html.

CHAPTER 6

Identifying the Underlying Business Imperatives and Drivers

The first and most important of the 10 principles presented in Chapter 4 is that the Knowledge Management (KM) implementation should be led by the needs of the organization. But what does this really mean? Exactly how can business needs lead the development of the KM strategy? To determine this, you need to work out what the key organizational drivers or imperatives for KM actually are; gathering data through interviews or through workshops as described in the previous chapter. It also means, for example, that IT (Information Technology) does not lead your KM program; IT supports your KM program and is a stakeholder and Governance Team participant.

You must also be careful not to express the business needs for KM in KM-speak, but in the language of the organization. So once you have identified the key organizational drivers, how do you describe them in organization-speak?

The Four Potential Focus Areas

There are four potential strategic focuses for KM, shown in Figure 6.1.

An Operational Excellence focus for KM aims to improve the internal practices and processes of the organization so that it operates better, faster, cheaper, safer, or cleaner. The crucial knowledge is that of the operational processes, and the KM strategy will be about ensuring

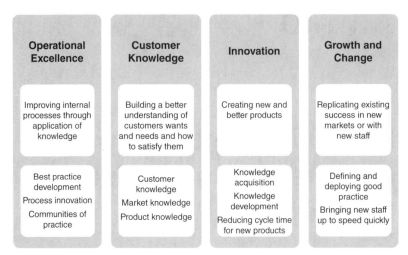

Figure 6.1   The four business focus areas for Knowledge Management

that these processes are as good as they can be throughout the organization. The majority of this knowledge will be internal (knowledge from within the organization). The strategy will include development and deployment of continually improving practices, process innovation, the use of communities of practice and knowledge bases, and standardization of process wherever possible. Regardless of what sector your organization operates in, it is likely that you are concerned about operational efficiency and effectiveness, which means that operational excellence, is a cornerstone of your KM strategy.

A Customer Knowledge focus for KM aims to improve the delivery of knowledge to the customer interface—the people who work with the customers on a day-to-day basis—so that customer relationships are maintained, service levels are high, and sales volumes are increased. In a not-for-profit or non-governmental organization, your "customers" are the beneficiaries of your programs. Similar ideas apply in this circumstance as in a for-profit organization. The crucial knowledge is that of the products or services that the organization offers, as well as knowledge about the customers themselves, the market, your competitors, and other participants in the sector. The majority of this knowledge will be internal with some external knowledge (knowledge from outside the organization) being needed to fully understand the client, the market/ environment, the competitors, and other participants in the sector. Your KM strategy will include the creation of a reliable knowledge base of products or services for use by your sales force, your service force or your call center, allied with close attention to customer relationship management (CRM). There may also be elements of your strategy focused on the processes of selling and bidding, as even the best product or service will not make money if you can't sell it. If your organization is in the service sector, or is largely concerned with marketing and selling, then customer knowledge is likely to be the cornerstone of your KM strategy.

Customer knowledge also applies to internal customers, for example the IT department's help desk for internal use. The help desk will need to be able to address employee technology issues based on what services and equipment the employee is using. There is less focus on sales and marketing in working with internal customer knowledge, but the other issues and concerns exist in this scenario too.

An Innovation focus for KM involves the creation of new knowledge in order to create new products and services. The crucial knowledge is knowledge of the base technology and of the marketplace. Much of this knowledge will be external, which is what primarily differentiates an innovation strategy from other KM Strategies. The strategy will include knowledge-creating activities such as business driven action learning, think tanks, deep dives and other creativity processes, as well as knowledge-gathering activities such as technology watch and market research. There may also be elements of your strategy focused on reducing the cycle time for new products, as even the best product will not make money if takes too long to get it to the market. If your company is in the high tech, bio-tech or pharmaceutical sectors, or any other sector with a focus on research and development and/or new products, then innovation is likely to be the cornerstone of your KM strategy.

A Growth and Change focus for KM involves replicating existing success in new markets or with new staff. It is critical to identify lessons learned and successful practices, so that good practices can be duplicated and mistakes learned from, and to transfer existing knowledge to new staff. New staff need to be integrated efficiently and effectively with adequate training and knowledge transfer so that they become valuable members of the team as quickly as possible. Regardless of what industry you are in, growth and dealing with changing market and organization conditions is often a consideration in your KM strategy.

Which of the Four Will Be Your Strategic Focus?

In reality, companies may have elements of all four focus areas. They may be concerned about operating their manufacturing plants efficiently, while also developing customer knowledge, and retaining a focus on creating new products. However the KM strategy should primarily address the most important of these four. Don't spread yourself too thin; don't try to do everything all at once. Instead pick the most important driver, and devote your attention to developing an effective KM solution which addresses this focus area.

Doers vs. Makers vs. Sellers; Process and Product

Some companies *do* things, some *make* things, and some *sell* things. Different organizational focus, different approach to KM. The *doers* are concerned with operational efficiency, the *makers* are concerned either with operational efficiency or product innovation (depending on the product and the market they are in) and the *sellers* are concerned with customer knowledge. Is your company primarily a doer, a maker, or a seller?

This is of course an oversimplification, and most organizations are a mix of doing and making, and all sell something, but the point is that depending on the market you are in and the type of product or service you have, you will have a different focus to your KM strategy. One of the main differences in KM Strategies is the amount of attention placed on practice knowledge vs. product knowledge.

The archetypal practice organization would be the Army. They don't make things or sell things; they do things, and their KM approach is all about the development and improvement of practice. They develop their doctrines, they develop communities of practice, and they focus on Operational Excellence and continual practice improvement. The same is true for the professional services sector and the oil and gas sector. In the case of the oil companies, selling the product requires little knowledge about oil (except for those few specialists concerned with selling crude oil to refineries), and the main focus for KM is on practice improvement. The KM framework involves communities of practice, best practices, practice owners and practice improvement.

A typical product-based maker organization would be an aircraft manufacturer or a car manufacturer. They exist to make things. Their KM approach is all about the development and improvement of product. They develop product guidelines for their engineers, their sales staff, and their service staff. At DaimlerChrysler, their Electronic Book of Knowledge was about automobile components, and their Tech Clubs were more communities of product than communities of practice. In a maker organization, the experts are more likely to be experts on a product than on a practice area. With the more complex products, where design knowledge is critical, KM can become Knowledge Based Engineering, with design rationale embedded into CAD files and other design products. The Air Force, in contrast to the Army, is focused primarily on product learning—learning about the airplane itself, much of which learning is shared with the aircraft manufacturer. For a product-based organization, the entire focus is on knowledge of product and product improvement.

The danger in KM comes when you try to impose a solution where it doesn't apply, for example imposing a maker KM solution onto a doer business, or an Operational Excellence KM solution onto an Innovation business. This is why we suggest you choose one area of focus for your KM strategy, and work with the parts of the business where that focus area is important.

Organizational Demographics

Another factor that can influence your KM strategy is the demographic composition of your workforce.

Take a Western engineering-based organization. Here the economy is static, and the population growth is stable. Engineering is not a "sexy" topic. The workforce is largely made up of baby boomers. A large proportion of the workforce is over 50, with many staff approaching retirement. Within the company there are very high levels of knowledge which is dispersed around the organization, scattered around many teams and locations. Communities of practice are important in a situation like this, so that people can ask each other for advice, and receive advice from anywhere. Experienced staff collaborate with each other to create new knowledge out of their shared expertise. The biggest risk to many Western engineering-based organizations is knowledge loss, as so many of the workforce will retire soon.

Compare this with a Far Eastern engineering-based organization. Here the economy is growing, the population is growing, there is a hunger for prosperity, and engineering is also a growth area. The workforce is predominantly young with many of them employed less than two years in the company. There are only a handful of real experts, and a host of inexperienced staff. Experience is a rare commodity, and is centralized within the company, retained within the centers of excellence, and the small expert groups. Here the issue is not collaboration, but rapid integration and enhanced training. The risk is not retention of knowledge, it is deployment of knowledge.

These two demographic profiles would lead you to take two different approaches to your KM strategy. The KM strategy for the Western company would introduce communities of practice, and use the dispersed expertise to collaborate on Operational Excellence, or on knowledge of customers and products. Knowledge bases could be used to harness the dispersed expertise. There would be huge potential for Innovation, as people reuse and build on ideas from each other. Crowdsourcing, and "asking the audience" are excellent strategies for finding knowledge, and Idea Jams would be a powerful way of innovating. There would be a strong strategic component of knowledge retention to the strategy. We describe a retention-based strategy in Chapter 18.

The Eastern engineering-based company, on the other hand, would focus on the development and deployment of standard practices and

Table 6.1   Knowledge Management core strategy as a function of demographics and strategic focus area

Demographic	Operational excellence	Customer knowledge	Innovation	Growth and Change
Aging workforce	Retention of operational knowledge to protect core operational capability	Retention of customer knowledge to protect core sales and relationships	Retention of innovative capability	Retention and deployment of operational and customer knowledge to protect core operational capability and sales relationships
Balanced workforce	Development and deployment of internal best practices and processes	Development and deployment of best knowledge of customers, market and product	Embedding Innovation processes, and creating diversity in teams	Development and deployment of internal best practices and processes as well as customer, market and product knowledge
Young workforce	Provision of basic and advanced operational knowledge to new and developing staff	Provision of basic and advanced product and customer knowledge to new and developing staff	Training in innovation, innovation processes, and creating as much diversity as possible in teams	Provision of basic and advanced operational, customer, and product knowledge to new and developing staff

procedures, and on developing and deploying capability among its youthful workforce. The experts would create first-rate training and educational material, and the focus would be on communities of learning rather than communities of practice. Widespread innovation would be discouraged until the staff had built enough experience to know which rules can be bent, and which must be adhered to. Crowd-sourcing is not a good strategy, and the "wisdom of the experts" is likely to trump the "wisdom of the crowd." When the (relatively few) experienced staff are at risk of departing, retention of knowledge is as much a part of your strategy as the development of capability among the younger workforce.

Demographic composition is one of the important factors that your KM strategy must address, namely the amount of expertise in the organ-ization, and how widely it is dispersed.

A Combination View

It is possible to combine the demographic view with the focus areas described previously. Table 6.1 suggests what your core KM strat-egy may be, based on a combination of the four focus areas and the two demographic types (with the addition of another demographic type, a balanced workforce with a good spread of young and experienced staff).

Example of Business Imperatives

An example of a clear business focus—cost reduction and operational efficiency, is given in the following section. This is from the *2011 KM Strategy for the Adaptation Fund*.[1] The business focus statements in the following section not only identify the business driver (operational effectiveness and cost) but show how KM can impact that driver, and how the KM program should be evaluated.

Overall Goal

11. The Fund will strive to improve the design and effec-tiveness of adaptation projects and programs by creating mechanisms that enable it to extract, analyze, learn and share lessons from the projects and programs it finances.

The Value of KM

15. The KM goal to increase the effectiveness of the Fund and its projects ultimately should lead to a reduction of costs. Ongoing measurement of the Fund's KM achievements will show that it is worth the investment. The Fund's KM program should be monitored and evaluated based on two criteria, efficiency and effectiveness:

Efficiency

- Capitalize on lessons learned to minimize errors and duplications in the design of new projects, and optimize the Fund's operational procedures
- Reduce the loss of knowledge once a Board member or a Secretariat staff leaves the job
- Reduce new staff/board member training time
- Improve donors' coordination
- Provide easy-to-retrieve information for users on the Web

Effectiveness

- Increase projects' capacity to effectively address adaptation issues
- Increase number of National Implementing Entities that submit applications
- Increase beneficiaries' satisfaction
- Generate new knowledge and data sets valuable for the adaptation community

Summary and Next Steps

Understanding the business drivers is crucial. KM needs to be driven by business needs and business imperatives, such as Operational Excellence (including elements of cost, time and quality), Customer Support, Innovation, or Growth and Change. The driver for you will depend on what type of organization you work for—a doer, a maker, or a seller—and on the demographics of the organization. Once you have a clear idea of the basic drivers, then it is time to move on to developing the vision for how KM will affect that driver.

Note

1. Adaptation Fund Board Ethics and Finance Committee, "Knowledge Management Strategy and Work Programme" (Bonn: Adaptation Fund, September 14, 2011), http://adaptation-fund.org/sites/default/files/AFB.EFC_.6.3%20Knowledge%20management%20strategy.pdf.

CHAPTER 7

Knowledge Management Vision and Scope

After completing one of the exercises at a training course in Stockholm, almost as an afterthought we mentioned Lord Browne's vision for Knowledge Management (KM), used extensively within BP, and quoted in his article "Unleashing the Power of Learning."[1] His vision was as follows:

> Most activities or tasks are not onetime events... Our philosophy is fairly simple:
>> Every time we do something again, we should do it better than the last time.

One of the participants came up to us afterwards and said that this had been an "Aha!" moment for him, and that this simple vision had, for him, graphically linked KM and business value.

This is the value of having a simple but powerful vision to support KM.

A vision like this is something everyone can buy into—nobody wants to do things worse than the last time!—because it explains *why* we are introducing KM; not for its own sake, but to focus on a specific business issue, the issue we referred to in Chapter 6 as Operational Excellence.

A vision like this also carries significant implications. In order to do things better than last time, we need to know *how* it was done last time, *what* was identified last time as improvement opportunities, and *how* these opportunities can be put into effect. We need a complete set of knowledge from "the last time" and then we need to innovate beyond this if necessary. And remember: "the last time" may have been in another country, or by another team, perhaps many years ago. Thus the vision requires a system of capturing knowledge from "the last time" and transferring it through time and space to "the next time" in order to improve performance.

A simply stated vision like Lord Browne's will be very powerful in communicating the KM strategy throughout your organization, by explaining the *why* behind KM.

Example Vision Statements

Here are a few other vision statements from companies. Some are official statements, some are CEO statements that encapsulate the vision, and some are statements crafted by the KM team. See which ones "speak" to you.

- "To create a world class knowledge-sharing culture and environment that contributes to Accenture's success." (Accenture)[2]

- "FTA knows what it knows; it is continuously filling the gaps of what it does not know. We have, therefore, increased the use of innovative approaches for accomplishing both our long-range planning and our day-to-day activities." (Federal Transit Administration of Ohio)[3]

- "Health Canada analyses, creates, shares and uses health knowledge to maintain and improve the health of the people of Canada:

  o through its KM processes and strategies which are tailored to advance the business lines of the department

  o as a model knowledge organization

  o as a leader, facilitator and partner, in the development of a Canadian health info-structure, responding to national and international trends and opportunities." (Health Canada)[4]

- "The focus of USAID's Knowledge Management Program is to connect people to the processes and technology that will help them to work effectively with partners to accomplish USAID's mission. The KM principles of knowledge capture, sharing and application helps the Agency to adapt to rapidly changing events by incorporating lessons learned and past experiences into decision-making and program planning decisions." (USAID)[5]

- "New Knowledge will be created, shared, and reused, as part of IAI personnel's common practice, for the achievement of IAI's vision and the fulfillment of its goal." (Israel Aircraft Industry)[6]

- "Knowing what we know, and knowing what we need to know. KM is about people working together to empower our people, to plan our future, to achieve our vision and mission of excellence, to champion sustainable development and productive partnerships. Strengthening how we manage our knowledge will make us more relevant and results oriented, efficient, integrated, productive and innovative." (Saudi Aramco)[7]

- "FAO will facilitate the access to and exchange of knowledge, as well as its generation, in the domain of agriculture and food security. It will assist its Members in generating, accessing and utilizing knowledge in food and agriculture, as well as any other knowledge that relates to it, required to address Members' individual and collective development and food security goals." (Food and Agriculture Organization of the United Nations)[8]

- "The vision of WHO KM is of global health equity through better KM and sharing." (World Health Organization)[9]

- "To support communications and advocacy efforts by Pacific nations for the best management of their Oceanic Fisheries resources." (Pacific Islands Oceanic Fisheries Management project)[10]

What Will Your Vision Statement Look Like?

The examples mentioned previously bring a whole range of approaches to the idea of a vision statement, but remember the purpose of your vision statement. It is to give people a flavor of what will be possible after KM has been introduced, expressed in terms of the value and/or purpose of the organization, and to distill this into something that can be easily remembered.

What you need is something memorable that encapsulates the purpose and values of KM within your organization. The statement should help people to see (hence the name "vision") what KM will make possible, and therefore why you are doing it. Three short sentences should be the maximum; when you need to draw breath halfway through a statement, it's too long.

Creating the Vision

A good process for creating a vision statement as part of a strategy workshop is to run a Pyramid Process exercise. This exercise should follow a discussion on the business drivers and business benefits, as listed in the agenda in Table 5.1. The Pyramid Process exercise works as follows:

- Ask each individual to draft a vision statement

    o Project yourself 5 years into the future, when KM is fully established and embedded in behaviors and culture

    o What will it be like? What value will it add?

- In two or three short sentences, using simple language, explain what KM will make possible

- Individuals join up into groups of four to six, and compare their vision statements. They draw the elements together into a common vision statement that the group can support. They should be careful not just to add everyone's vision together, but should synthesize and summarize

- Then all groups come together, and draw the elements into a common vision statement. If this ends up too long and complex, use a vote to decide which parts to cut out so the vision can be simplified

- Ensure that the vision remains clear. If you end with platitudes, challenge the group to clarify what the real vision is

If you are compiling a vision statement from the results of many interviews instead of convening a strategy workshop, then go through the responses received at the interviews and look for the common words, the common word pairings, the common verbs, the common thoughts, and find a way to bring these together. One way to do this is to create a Wordle (word cloud) from the input you have received, and then use the prominent words to craft a vision statement. Another approach is to write the key words and word pairings onto cards, and sort these into a vision that makes sense. The risk here is that you will end up with something bland and uninspiring, which everyone can support but nobody is enthused by, and you may need to inject some creativity yourself to come up with a powerful statement.

Your final option, which is often the best option, is to take all the input you have been given and craft something that takes the spirit of what you have received, and turn it into something simple and compelling. Test it with your sponsor, and steering team (if you have one), and on a focus group of representative staff. Then publish!

Defining the Scope

Together with defining the vision comes defining the scope. As we discussed in Chapter 1, KM is such a broad topic that you cannot possibly address it all, and a very early conversation will be to discuss with your manager what is in scope, and what is out of scope.

Your scope statement should define:

- The areas of KM you will address
- The areas of KM you will not address
- The areas of the organization you will address (e.g. all operation units? All geographies?)
- Who will be involved in your KM activities; whether your KM strategy will apply to just organizational staff, or organizational staff and contractors, or the general public, or customers

The conversations with your manager, as we recommended in Chapter 1, will have given you a broad view of the scope. The data you have gathered on critical knowledge areas will help you refine this, as the scope of the strategy should be broad enough to cover the areas of critical knowledge, and the staff, business units, business processes, and KM elements which will be needed to address them.

Example Scope Statements

The following, from the KM Strategy of the South Yorkshire Fire and Rescue service[11], is an excellent example of a scope statement.

> The strategy covers all personnel employed by SYFR, all information generated within the organization, and it will utilize SYFR ICT and other assets as appropriate.
>
> Knowledge may be gained from the broader fire service community, and as part of the strategy SYFR will proactively scan the external environment for relevant upcoming national and international developments, as well as best practice.
>
> Regarding knowledge gained from the wider public, sharing structured feedback from various public consultation exercises will also provide valuable new sources. In addition to our own surveys, collaborative knowledge sharing may be developed with partner organizations where appropriate, and subject to information sharing protocols and data protection legislation. For example, from autumn 2008 local authorities will be running new Placed Based Surveys to gather important information about the needs and views of communities. The results of these surveys will start to become available to public services in the spring of 2009.
>
> Staff involved in frontline interactions with the public will also be encouraged to feedback views and comments expressed verbally to them during the course of their duties.

The World Health Organization 2005 KM Strategy[12] defines the scope of the document in time-bounded terms, as well as the people who will be affected by the strategy, as follows:

> This strategy serves as the framework for establishing the program of work for the WHO KM team, consisting of

headquarters, regions and country programs working in the area of KM and sharing. It responds to the need for equitable access to knowledge, and for broader application of evidence in public health. This document sets out a medium-term strategy and its rationale and approach. The strategy will be reassessed in 2007.

Summary and Next Steps

The vision explains *why* KM is being introduced and the scope defines *what* Knowledge Management will cover. Both of these need to be clearly articulated and agreed, as a starting point to the rest of the strategy. Once the vision and scope are agreed you can move on to defining the strategic knowledge areas on which the strategy will focus.

Notes

1. John Browne and Steven E. Prokesh, "Unleashing the Power of Learning: An Interview with British Petroleum's John Browne," *Harvard Business Review* 75, no. 5 (September 1997): 146–68.

2. Jongsung Lee, "Knowledge Management at Accenture" (Richard Ivey School of Business, 1997), 9, www.slideshare.net/sekretnay/knowledge-management-at-accenture.

3. Susan Camarena, "Knowledge Management in FTA: The first two years….," presentation at the Ohio Transportation Engineering Conference, October 2009, 9, www.dot.state.oh.us/engineering/OTEC/2008%20Presentations/35B.pdf.

4. Health Canada, "Vision and Strategy for Knowledge Management and IM/IT for Health Canada" (Ottawa: Health Canada, December 1998), 2, www.providersedge.com/docs/km_articles/Health_Canada's_Vision_and_Strategy_for_KM.pdf.

5. USAID, *Knowledge Management Support,* last updated: March 18, 2014, www.usaid.gov/results-and-data/information-resources/knowledge-management-support.

6. Rony Dayan, Edna Pasher, and Ron Dvir, "The Knowledge Management Journey of Israel Aircraft Industry." In A. S. Kazi and P. Wolf, eds., *Real-Life Knowledge Management: Lessons from the Field* (Finland: KnowledgeBoard, 2006). www.innovationecology.com/papers/IAI%20case%20knowledgeboard%20ebook.pdf.

7. Hamid Rowaihy, "A KM Vision," Saudi Aramco, www.youtube.com/watch?v=KQbpmIlu4w0.

8. Food and Agriculture Organization of the United Nations, FAO Knowledge Strategy (Rome: FAO, March 2011), www.fao.org/fileadmin/user_upload/capacity_building/KM_Strategy.pdf.

9. World Health Organization, Knowledge Management Strategy (Geneva: World Health Organization, 2005), 9, WHO/EIP/KMS/2005, www.who.int/kms/about/strategy/kms_strategy.pdf.

10. Lisa Williams-Lahari, Knowledge Management Strategy (Pacific Islands Oceanic Fisheries Management (OFM) project, Honiara, Solomon Islands, draft: October 2007), www.ffa.int/gef/files/gef/OFMP%20Knowledge%20Management%20Strategy.pdf.

11. South Yorkshire Fire and Rescue, "Knowledge Management Strategy 2008-2011 – Appendix 1," *Knowledge Management Strategy* v. 0.2 (March 2008), www.docstoc.com/docs/69812138/Knowledge-Management-Strategy—SOUTH-YORKSHIRE-FIRE-AND-RESCUE.

12. World Health Organization, Knowledge Management Strategy (Geneva: World Health Organization, 2005), WHO/EIP/KMS/2005.1, www.who.int/kms/about/strategy/kms_strategy.pdf.

CHAPTER 8

Strategic Knowledge Areas

As consultants, one of the greatest Knowledge Management (KM) insights, and one of the best pieces of news we bring to client organizations is this: "You don't have to manage it all."

Why is this a great piece of news? Because if you think about managing only your critical organizational knowledge it gives you a real strategic focus and a place to start. That's why focusing on critical knowledge is listed as one of the ten principles in Chapter 4.

We frequently find that when people embark upon implementing KM, they begin by thinking about the solution itself. They may research technology, they may seek out some excellent processes, they may (if they are smart) think about the roles and accountabilities the organization will need, and they may contemplate the use of communities of practice, global task forces, virtual teams, blogs, wikis, and any other of the fashionable solutions that are popular in the market place. However the piece of thinking that we find often *doesn't* happen this early in the process is the thinking about "What Knowledge."

What knowledge needs to be managed?

Exactly what knowledge do we need to flow around the organization? What's the high value knowledge and know-how? What's the knowledge that will give the organization a competitive edge? What is the knowledge that will deliver "first learner advantage"?

Our assertion is that if you focus your strategy proactively on the topics of highest business value, then your KM implementation will not only be easier, it will deliver far higher benefit. We call these topics of highest business value "strategic knowledge areas."

We can define a strategic knowledge area as a knowledge topic that is of primary importance to the business, representing knowledge and know-how that supports delivery of the business strategy, and where KM can therefore deliver the greatest strategic value.

Your KM strategy should identify the strategic knowledge areas and use them as focus points.

In the 1990s, the BP KM strategy was clearly focused on what we called areas of "knowledge intensity"; areas where knowledge had a real impact on the way work was done, and thus where KM had the greatest potential for impacting business results. If you focus your KM implementation to address these areas, you will not only deliver value to the organization, you will also solve difficult issues for the business unit's executives. Linda Davies, former head of KM at Mars, likened solving pain-points for high-level executives to "taking the thorn out of the lion's paw," the story from the old fable where Androcles relieved the lion's pain, and was later to find the lion to be a vital ally at a time of need.[1] Davies focused her implementation on strategic knowledge areas, and found that successfully delivering the strategic knowledge gained her support and sponsorship from senior management when she needed it.

Identifying the Strategic Knowledge Areas

How do you find these strategic topics, to become the focus for your Knowledge Management strategy? Basically there are two approaches: top-down, and bottom-up, and you should use both.

Top-down Approach

In the top-down approach you work downward from the business strategy, to the strategic activities that support it, and to the knowledge required to deliver the activities.

For example, if your strategy is inorganic growth, then the key activities are mergers, acquisitions and integration, and the strategic knowledge topics are how to merge, how to acquire and how to integrate. If your strategy is to increase market share, then the activities will involve marketing and selling, and crucial knowledge will be how to market, how to sell, and how to understand the customer. Often, people can be a little bit more specific—perhaps the crucial knowledge is selling through a dealer network, or online marketing, or selling to key accounts. Whatever the topic, you can link it back through activity to business strategy. To identify your critical knowledge areas through a top-down model, choose a selection of operational business unit leaders, and ask them to identify the key knowledge which, if they had it, would significantly help in delivering their business strategy. Ask them what it is that they don't know but wish they did. What are the business "I don't knows" that are keeping them awake at night?

You might get answers like these:

- I wish we knew how to…

  o Sell chocolate in rural China

  o Halve the water use in my brewery

  o Close down, maintain, and start up my refinery in just three weeks

  o Avoid agglomerates in my polyethylene plant

  o Reduce my well costs by 25%, and still drill safely

  o Sell long-term service contracts that make us money

  o Be more efficient in our program delivery to have a greater economic impact in the region

These are strategic knowledge areas from a range of real organizations.

Figure 8.1   Top-down approach to identifying critical knowledge areas

An alternative and more structured approach to getting such answers from senior managers is to start from the business strategy, and work downward, as shown in Figure 8.1.

Asxk your senior managers:

- "What is the core operational strategy for your part of the business?"

- Then ask, "What do we need to be able to do (i.e. what competencies do we need) in order to deliver our strategy?"

- Then ask "What do we need to know to be competent?"

The answer to that third question identifies the critical knowledge which drives your KM strategy.

As you identify these strategic knowledge topics, you need to understand the nature of the topic. Important questions to ask are:

- If we had this knowledge, how much of a business difference might it make?

- Do we have this knowledge in-house already or will we need to acquire it? Where is the knowledge now?

- How widespread is this knowledge in the organization at the moment? How widespread does it need to be?

- How mature is the topic? Is it brand new knowledge, or is it a well-established field?

Bottom-up Approach

At the same time, you can take a bottom-up approach and survey the knowledge workers in the organization. Ask them a similar question: "What is the crucial knowledge that you wish you had, to help you do your job better?" Try to focus, if possible, on know-how rather than on specific pieces of information. You are looking for answers such as "We need to know how to rapidly and effectively integrate with a company we have just merged with" rather than "I wish I knew who our next merger target will be" or "We need to have a list of staff in the other company."

The answer you receive will obviously depend on the role of the individual you ask. If you ask people from the marketing department then you will get a list of marketing knowledge topics. If you ask the sales staff you will get a list of the sales topics. If you ask the finance department then it will be finance topics. In a way, these are more tactical knowledge areas than strategic knowledge areas, but you can combine them with the top-down answers, and use them to sense check and calibrate those top-down answers. As you move into KM implementation, the knowledge workers in the business will be among your key stakeholders; you will need to satisfy their knowledge needs as well as those of senior managers. By engaging them at this early stage you will have included their requirements in the KM strategy, which helps ensure their buy-in and support later in the implementation process.

Ranking the Importance of Your Strategic Knowledge Areas

Whether you work from the top down or the bottom up, or a combination of the two, you will identify far more strategic knowledge areas than you can focus on in the short term. You therefore will need to rank them in some order of priority. There are two dimensions to identifying the high priority strategic knowledge areas, at least in terms of steering your KM strategy: importance to the organization and urgency.

You can assess these issues as part of your top-down data gathering, or at a separate workshop with some of the senior managers.

The importance dimension can be addressed by asking what the consequences would be if the knowledge of each strategic area was lost or diminished. What would be the impact on the business?

Urgency is a little more difficult to gauge. There are at least four cases where knowledge can be in need of urgent attention:

- Where knowledge is important to the organization, but you don't have it (or don't have enough of it). Here the focus will be on the acquisition and development of knowledge—on innovation, knowledge creation, research, and action learning.

- Where knowledge exists widely in the organization, but is in silos, and not shared, or otherwise not properly managed. Here knowledge is used inefficiently—advances in one part of the business are not shared and learned from in other parts of the business. Multiple, and inefficient, solutions exist, where one or two solutions would be better. Here the focus will be on the elements of knowledge sharing, and knowledge improvement, such as communities of practice, lessons learned, and development of knowledge assets, best practices, and standardization.

- Where important knowledge is at risk of loss, perhaps through the retirement of key members of staff. Here the focus must be on developing and deploying a retention strategy.

- When critical knowledge is held by a contractor, partner, or supplier, and they don't have KM. Here the focus is on defining a KM framework for them to apply, to keep your knowledge safe.

As part of your top-down interviews you will have gathered the data to answer these questions.

Those important and urgent knowledge issues are the ones that should drive your KM strategy, as you tackle them one by one.

The Strategy Map: Showing the Link to Business Strategy

A strategy map[2] is a pretty well established way of mapping out the strategy of an organization in a visual way. The standard Kaplan map starts with the organization's vision at the top of the page, and works down, via elements of the strategy, to the financial, customer, process and learning activities or objectives that support it (Figure 8.2).

KM should be aligned with this strategy map. As we know, KM should be driven by the organization's vision and strategy, and should support the key activities that are needed to deliver that strategy. When Kaplan and Norton developed the ideas around strategy maps KM was in its infancy and the learning activities or objectives they included were fairly generic. What KM can do is make these learning activities less generic, linking them to specific KM interventions and activities thus showing how the elements of KM directly support the business strategy.

In Figure 8.2, we have added a KM layer to a strategy map; in this case a fictional example map from a company building hospitals. The

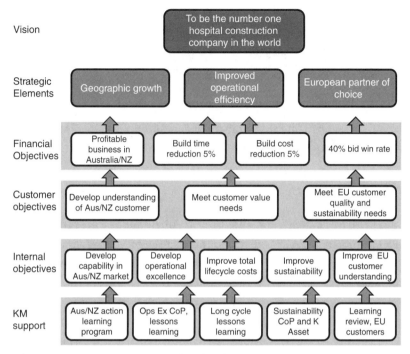

Figure 8.2   Strategy map with added KM layer

corporate vision "to be number one" is supported by the three strategic elements of growth, operational efficiency and customer relationships. KM can support the activities that flow down from each strategic element, and the strategy map shows this in a very visual way.

The two advantages of this form of strategic map are that it helps the KM team to focus on the interventions that most directly support business strategy, and that it makes it clear to the business how KM will help in delivering the strategy.

Examples of Strategic Knowledge Areas

It is surprising how few of the published KM strategies available on the internet identify areas of critical knowledge that form a focus for their strategy. The majority of the strategies seem to have no focus at all. Here are some rare exceptions.

From the KM Strategy for the African Development Bank:[3]

> The KM strategy proposes three interrelated areas of focus for the next 5 years. . . . These thematic areas include
>
> - poverty reduction and equity
> - enhancing the competitiveness and productivity of African economies
> - improving the quality of institutions and economic management

The KM strategy for the International Fund for Agricultural Development (IFAD)[4] identifies four areas of critical knowledge, from which it will select two to act as pilots. The relevant text is as follows.

> At the headquarters level, building on the existing thematic groups, IFAD will initially develop two thematic networks, choosing from among the themes of
>
> - gender
> - rural finance
> - natural resources management
> - indigenous peoples
>
> The networks will serve as laboratories for systematic learning by IFAD on the linking of knowledge development at the local, regional and corporate levels with IFAD's policy. They should better position IFAD to distill knowledge and experience through such processes as best-practice reviews and the IFAD Policy Forum, and share knowledge through Learning Notes and informal knowledge-sharing for use in policy dialogue, program development and implementation activities.

Summary and Next Steps

Not all knowledge is of equal value, and not all knowledge needs to be addressed as part of your KM strategy. Determine the strategic knowledge areas—either through a top-down or a bottom-up process using a strategy map to display this visually. These knowledge areas will provide focus for your strategy. Once the strategic knowledge areas have been identified you can move on to the next topic: an assessment of the current state.

Notes

1. Aesop, "Androcles," trans. G. F. Townsend, classiclit.about.com/library/bl-etexts/aesop/bl-aesop-androcles.htm.

2. Robert S. Kaplan and David P. Norton, *Strategy Maps: Converting Intangible Assets Into Tangible Outcomes* (Boston: Harvard Business Press, 2004).

3. African Development Bank, "Revised Bank Knowledge Management and Development Strategy 2008-2012" (Tunis: African Development Bank, 2007), http://www.afdb.org/fileadmin/uploads/afdb/Documents/Policy-Documents/10000001-EN-REVISED-BANK-KNOWLEDGE-MANAGEMENT-AND-DEVLOPMENT-STRATEGY-2008-2012.PDF.

4. International Fund for Agricultural Development, "Knowledge Management: Strategy" (Rome: IFAD, 2007), http://www.ifad.org/pub/policy/km/e.pdf.

CHAPTER 9

Assessing the Current State of KM in the Organization

Once you have determined the organizational drivers for Knowledge Management and the critical knowledge that needs to be managed, you need to assess the current state of KM in the organization by answering the following questions:

- Why is this knowledge not being managed already?

- What is preventing knowledge flowing from the people who have it to the people who need it?

- What are the most important things we can do to unblock, or to facilitate, this flow of knowledge?

In other words, you need to assess the current state, to see what changes are needed to bring in KM. At the same time you can identify the current strengths and the current successful areas, which can be built upon in order to construct a complete KM framework.

In order to assess the current state of KM, you need an assessment model. There are many models available, and every KM consultancy offers its own version. These models usually contain a list of key elements for the success of KM, and allow you to measure the strength of these elements. You are free to take any of these models—all provide a good overview of the state of KM in your organization—but a better approach is to assess against a robust framework template, which will also be the template for the draft KM framework you will build in Chapter 10.

We suggest that the assessment and the framework be fully aligned and address a comprehensive set of KM flow components, and a comprehensive set of enablers.

The four commonly recognized components of knowledge flow are those recognized by Nonaka and Takeuchi[1], often referred to as the SECI model:

- Socialization—the transfer of knowledge from person to person through communication

- Externalization—the documentation of tacit knowledge

- Combination—compiling, synthesizing and organizing captured or documented knowledge

- Internalization—interacting with explicit knowledge in order to understand and integrate it into your thinking

These are all generic components of knowledge flow, and you need all of them to be working in your organization. You need to be connecting people, so they can talk and discuss and share knowledge through conversation. You need to be capturing knowledge which can and should be captured. You need to be synthesizing and organizing this knowledge. And you need to be paying attention to how people find, read, learn and inwardly digest that knowledge.

The three commonly recognized enablers for KM are as follows, with a fourth of our own:

- People (and in the context of a management framework, this means roles and accountabilities)

- Processes

- Technology

- We also add a fourth component: the enabler of governance—governance being all those activities which influence behavior within an organization. We described the principle of including governance within the KM framework in Chapter 4, where we explained that governance covers the three elements of clear expectations, performance management, and support.

When conducting an assessment of the current state, combine the four components of knowledge flow with the four enablers to create 16 sets of questions, which should be asked in the context of the organizational drivers and the critical knowledge areas.

Assessment Questions

The following list of assessment questions is recommended in order to achieve an accurate evaluation of the current state of KM-related activities in the organization.

1. What roles, resources and accountabilities exist in the organization to facilitate direct conversations or discussions for exchanging critical knowledge? How effective are they in achieving this? How could they be improved? What is missing?

2. What processes do you already have for dialogue and discussion for exchanging critical knowledge? How well do these processes work? How could the processes be improved? What is missing?

3. What technologies do you already have to facilitate direct conversations or discussions for exchanging critical knowledge? How well do these work? How could they be improved? What is missing?

4. What governance do you already have concerning these direct conversations or discussions for exchanging critical knowledge? What expectations, policies, performance management, reward and recognition, and support are in place? How well do these work? How could they be improved? What is missing?

5. What roles, resources and accountabilities exist in the organization to facilitate capture and documentation of critical knowledge? How effective are they in achieving this? How could they be improved? What is missing?

6. What processes do you already have for capture and documentation of critical knowledge? How well do these processes work? How could the processes be improved? What is missing?

7. What technologies do you already have to facilitate capture and documentation of critical knowledge? How well do these work? How could they be improved? What is missing?

8. What governance do you already have concerning knowledge capture? What expectations, policies, performance management, reward and recognition, and support are in place? How well do these work? How could they be improved? What is missing?

9. What roles, resources and accountabilities exist in the organization for compiling, synthesizing and organizing critical knowledge? How effective are they in achieving this? How could they be improved? What is missing?

10. What processes do you already have for compiling, synthesizing and organizing critical knowledge? How well do these processes work? How could the processes be improved? What is missing?

11. What technologies do you already have to facilitate compiling, synthesizing and organizing critical knowledge? How well do these work? How could they be improved? What is missing?

12. What governance do you already have concerning compiling, synthesizing and organizing critical knowledge? What expectations, policies, performance management, reward and recognition, and support are in place? How well do these work? How could they be improved? What is missing?

13. What roles, resources and accountabilities exist in the organization for ensuring critical knowledge is sought, found, read/viewed and internalized? How effective are they in achieving this? How could they be improved? What is missing?

14. What processes do you already have for ensuring critical knowledge is sought, found, read/viewed and internalized? How well do these processes work? How could the processes be improved? What is missing?

15. What technologies do you already have to enable seeking, finding, reading/viewing and internalizing critical knowledge? How well do these work? How could they be improved? What is missing?

16. What governance do you already have concerning seeking, finding, reading/viewing and internalizing critical knowledge? What expectations, policies, performance management, reward and recognition, and support are in place? How well do these work? How could they be improved? What is missing?

Assessment Process

It is particularly useful to involve external objective experienced people in the assessment process part of setting your strategy. Self-assessment is a bit like self-diagnosis for a medical condition—you may get it right but you might get it wrong, or (even more likely) you might miss some less obvious symptoms. Better to go to experienced professionals if you can. They will know the things you don't know, and will even be aware of your "blind spots"—the things you don't know that you don't know.

If you cannot find such experienced objective people, then you have two options:

1. You can convene a workshop with a representative selection of people from the organization and go through the questions one by one. It will probably take a full day to address all of the questions in detail.

2. You can hold a series of one-on-one interviews with a representative selection of people from the organization, and go through the questions one by one. Each interview is likely to last an hour or two.

What to Do With the Results

You conduct the assessment to look for the missing factors and evaluate what the results are telling you. For example, if you have plenty of processes and technology but few roles and accountabilities, then part of your KM strategy will be to assign accountabilities and appoint roles for facilitating the flow of critical knowledge. If the elements are in place for externalization and combination, but not for socialization or internalization, then your strategy should focus on these two elements. If governance is absent, then your strategy must address the introduction of governance elements. The final aim is to have a complete framework in place for your critical knowledge, and the strategy will focus on filling in the gaps.

Another way to organize the output from the strategy workshop(s) and interview(s) is to create a SWOT analysis table. SWOT refers to Strengths, Weaknesses, Opportunities, and Threats. Strengths and weaknesses are internal factors, so they are things that the organization has direct control over, and the majority of your results will fall into these two areas. Opportunities and threats are external factors; they are things that are going on in the external environment that at best the organization has only indirect control over.

A SWOT analysis can help focus in on themes that emerge from your workshops and interviews. It can highlight things that are working well, and things that aren't, but also where there are opportunities and threats from external factors that need to be considered in constructing your strategy.

Examples

The following are KM current state assessment examples from Health Canada and the eThekwini Municipality in South Africa; they provide some insight into what some organizations are like when they start their KM programs.

The 1998 Health Canada KM strategy[2] has a simple but rather bleak overview of the current state, suggesting that they were starting from a relatively low state.

> The Status Quo—At Health Canada we do not:
>
> - know what our employees know
>
> - know what information we have
>
> - know what information we need
>
> - have a coordinated approach to the capturing of employees' knowledge
>
> - have a guiding blueprint for investments in knowledge, information, applications or technology.

The KM Strategy of the eThekwini Municipality in South Africa[3] used the results of a commissioned study into the current KM status, and concluded:

> 1. The structure and location of KM units in local government seem to be an overwhelming concern for all

developing KM projects. In many instances if KM did not have a physical presence in the official organogram of the municipality, it got little regard in terms of resources and support.

2. At least two of the initiatives sampled expressed frustration at not being able to sufficiently convince senior managers and politicians of the role that KM could play in improving the efficiency and productivity of the institution.

3. Where KM unit deliverables had not been integrated into the core business of the municipality, the value of the unit remained marginal. This had been the experience of both the Joburg and the Mangaung units. KM Units that had focused solely on project needs also ran the risk of becoming obsolete once that city program had run its course. It seemed that the ideal model would be somewhere between developing independent capacity and playing a role in City programs.

4. In some cases there seems to be an over reliance on web based tools as a solution for knowledge gathering and dissemination. While ICT can play a very valuable role in a comprehensive KM plan, it should be seen as an enabler where existing systems and processes are already in place. If tools are not properly integrated and accepted into the work practice of an institution, the intervention might end up being a white elephant.

Summary and Next Steps

Once you have a vision, then an assessment of the current state will tell you not only how far you are from that vision, but also what needs to be fixed. In this chapter we have given you a framework and a methodology for assessment. Once your assessment is complete you will be in a good position to move to the next step, namely defining the KM framework that will need to be introduced to your organization if the vision is to become reality for the areas of strategic knowledge.

Notes

1. Ikujiro Nonaka and Hirotaka Takeuchi, *The Knowledge-Creating Company: How Japanese Companies Create the Dynamics of Innovation,* (New York: Oxford University Press, 1995).

2. Health Canada, "Vision and Strategy for Knowledge Management and IM/IT for Health Canada" (Ottawa: Health Canada, December 1998), accessed May 29, 2014, www.providersedge.com/docs/km_articles/Health_Canada's_Vision_and_Strategy_for_KM.pdf.

3. Municipal Institute of Learning, "eThekwini Knowledge Strategy and Implementation Plan 2010–2014" (Durban, South Africa: MILE, November 2011), accessed May 29, 2014, http://www.mile.org.za/Come_Learn/Knowledge_Management/Knowledge%20Management%20Strategy/KM%20Strategy/KM%20Strategy.pdf.

Chapter 10

Knowledge Management Framework

In Chapter 9, we described a set of 16 questions for assessing the current state of Knowledge Management for your organization. Those questions were a combination of the four elements of socialization, externalization, combination, and internalization with the four enablers of people, process, technology, and governance. These same 16 possible combinations will form the components of the KM framework that we describe in this chapter.

However before we start work on the details of the framework, let's talk for a little bit about why KM needs a management framework at all.

The Need for a Knowledge Management Framework

The fourth of the ten principles listed in Chapter 4 is that the endgame for KM implementation will be to introduce a complete management framework for KM. We have already explained that there are many elements to KM. There is Connect and Collect, as we discussed in Chapter 1. There are the four elements of socialization, externalization, combination and internalization, as we discussed in Chapter 9. There are the four enablers of people (roles and accountabilities), processes, technologies, and governance, also covered in Chapter 9. The management framework for KM is the combination of these elements into a system, and that system is tailored and designed for your own organization.

All too often, KM implementations focus on just one element, and assume that will work in isolation. A common assumption, for example, is that knowledge has to be captured and published, which may lead you to focus on Collecting and not Connecting, Pushing and not Pulling, and Technology without process, roles, or governance. We described just such an unbalanced approach in Chapter 1.

Another common assumption is that all you have to do is introduce the technology to "let people talk" and knowledge will "share itself." With this assumption in place, you may focus on Connect, Push, and Technology, only to find that knowledge doesn't "share itself." The organization then wonders what went wrong; often blaming the technology, when in actual fact is was the lack of governance, roles, and Pull.

Taking a small element of KM and assuming it will work in isolation is like taking one ingredient and assuming it will create the whole recipe, or like taking one small element of a central heating system and assuming it will heat the house.

One common reason why KM consultants get hired by organizations is because they were disappointed by the results of a partially-implemented KM. "We had a KM program last year, we bought a new search engine, but people aren't using it," for example. Or "We introduced SharePoint and set up 40 communities of practice, but they are all inactive." "We put in place a lessons learned process, but we are just learning the same lessons over and over." The organization introduced a tool or a process or a technology, when what they needed was a complete KM framework.

Defining the Framework within the Strategy

Within your KM strategy document, you don't need to have worked out the components of the framework in detail, because you will test these components during piloting. However, you need to have a high-level framework design in mind in order to know what to pilot and what to test. Within the strategy document you can present the framework as a draft or outline in order to make it clear that more testing and verification of the framework will be needed. You are not defining how KM will operate in your organization, you are providing a model of how it might operate, which you will then pilot prior to roll-out.

The Questions You Need to Answer in Order to Define the Framework

In order to define the details of the Knowledge Management framework, you need to answer a number of questions. The answers to the questions will form the 16 components of the framework shown in Table 10.1. In this chapter we discuss these components in four sections, each one addressing one of the four enablers: people, process, technology, and governance. Once you have answered all of the questions in the following sections, you will have defined your draft framework.

People and Accountabilities

What roles and accountabilities will you have in the organization for promoting, facilitating, and ensuring transfer of knowledge through conversation? Will you be introducing communities of practice, for example, with roles such as the community leader, community facilitator and community sponsor?

What roles and accountabilities will you have in the organization for ensuring the capture of critical organizational knowledge? Who will be accountable within the projects, for example, or within the departments, or within the sales teams? Would you need additional roles? Or can you assign responsibilities to roles that already exist? And who is accountable for knowledge retention when knowledgeable people retire or leave the organization?

Table 10.1   Knowledge Management Framework

	Socialization	Externalization	Combination	Internalization
People				
Process				
Technology				
Governance				

What roles and accountabilities will you have in the organization for combining knowledge, and for looking after the explicit knowledge? These are the roles that you might call the "knowledge owner" roles, the people who combine and collate and synthesize knowledge into "knowledge assets" that others can use. Will this be done by the communities of practice, or by the process owners, or by the technical specialists, or by the subject matter experts, or by the functional departments? Somebody has to do this; somebody has to own, or steward, the knowledge of the organization; you need to put forward some thoughts at this stage about who this might be.

What roles and accountabilities will you have in the organization for ensuring that existing knowledge is sought, reviewed, and where applicable reused in operational activity? Who, in the projects, will be accountable for ensuring the past lessons are incorporated into project plans? Who, in operations, will be accountable for ensuring that best practices are reviewed and followed? Who will be accountable for ensuring that new staff are rapidly brought up to speed, and give them the knowledge they need?

Note that there may be some individuals or job posts that will cover more than one of these accountabilities. The leader of a community of practice, for example, may also be a knowledge owner.

Processes

What processes will you use for exchange of knowledge through communication? Will you need online communication, such as question and answer, online collaboration, or online discussion? Will you need face-to-face processes such as peer assist, knowledge café, knowledge exchange, or story telling circles? If so, how would you build these processes into your working systems, such as the operational cycle, or the project framework?

What processes will you use for the capture and documentation of knowledge? Will you require lesson-identification processes such as after-action reviews, retrospects, Kaizen, or quality circles? How would you build these processes into your working systems, such as the operational cycle, or the project framework? What processes will you use for the capture and documentation of knowledge when people retire, leave, or move jobs?

What processes will you use for the organization of knowledge? How will new knowledge be reviewed, validated, synthesized, incorporated into knowledge assets? How will the knowledge assets themselves be constructed and validated? How will existing knowledge be kept up to date?

What processes will you use for the review of existing knowledge, so that it can be targeted for reuse? Will there be a defined process, for example, where project teams get together, and look at past lessons and decide which ones to act on? Will there be a process where operation teams regularly review new practices and process improvements, and decide which ones to adopt?

Technology

What technology will support the transfer of knowledge through discussion and conversation? Will you need an "expertise finder" or "Yellow Pages" software, so you can rapidly find people with relevant skills? Will you need online discussion forums? Will you need social media technology?

What technology will you need to support the documentation of new knowledge? Will you need electronic notebooks, video recording, lessons databases, or lessons management systems, or blogging software?

What technology will you need to support the knowledge base? Will you need wikis, portals, or intranets?

What technology will you need to support the finding and reuse of knowledge? Will you need search, semantic search, RSS, subscribe-and-publish facilities?

Note that some of these technologies perform more than one of these tasks. You can find a description of technology options in Chapter 12.

Governance

The strategy stage of KM implementation is usually too soon to fully define the details of governance for each of the knowledge flow elements, which will not be completely understood until after piloting.

However, we recommend you start thinking about some of the higher level questions, such as the ones that follow.

What support mechanisms are you going to need for KM, both during the implementation stage, and after implementation is over? What size of KM support team will you need in these two stages?

When will you need a KM policy? Who is going to own it and write it? How will adherence to the policy requirements be monitored?

What sort of reporting system will you need for KM, and who are you going to report to, both during the implementation stage and once the implementation has been completed? What metrics will you collect and report?

What sort of performance management scheme might you need for KM; both during the implementation stage and once the implementation is completed? How will you recognize or incentivize the good performers? What will you do about the people who do not comply with the KM Policy?

How Do You Find the Answers to These Questions?

There are a number of ways to find the answers to these questions:

First, you will have reviewed all of these areas and components during the assessment phase. If you find any components that are already working reasonably well in your organization then keep them. Even if they're not perfect, keep them. It is far better to build the KM framework around things that already exist than to bring in everything new.

Second, this is another very good point at which to consider using the advice of an experienced professional. An experienced KM consultant will have seen many organizations like yours, and he or she will have a thorough understanding of the framework elements that should be suitable for your context. If you made use of external objective experienced people to help with the assessment, they will be ideally placed to advise you how to define your KM framework.

Third, benchmark yourself against organizations similar to yours. Find the ones that have successfully implemented a KM strategy, and look at the design of their KM framework. There may be framework elements that you can copy or adapt. Remember though that each organization must develop a framework that fits their context and their needs. Your framework will be unique to you.

Finally, talk with the people who own the internal processes and with people in the internal functions to get their opinions. Bounce your ideas off them, and listen to what they have to say. Talk to the people who own the project management framework, the operational management framework, and the performance management framework to see how KM processes can be embedded, and where the accountabilities might lie. Talk to IT about technology; they may already have some strategic views you can align with. Reassure them that you are not asking them to commit to anything at this stage, you are just asking for their views.

Framework Examples

Most of the public domain published KM strategies describe some sort of framework, though few of them describe it in much detail. Figure 10.1 depicts a framework presented by NASA in their 2002 Strategic Plan for Knowledge Management. It contains elements of people, process, technology, and supporting activities (some of which are governance elements). Illustrating the framework with an image helps people to quickly understand how the various components and activities fit together to create a cohesive whole.[1]

Sharing and Using Knowledge		
People	**Process**	**Technology**
• Enable remote collaboration • Support communities of practice • Reward and recognize knowledge sharing • Encourage storytelling	• Enhance knowledge capture • Manage information	• Enhance system integration and data mining • Utilize intelligent agents • Exploit expert systems
Supporting Activities		
Education and Training	Integrated Financial Management	IT Infrastructure	Human Resources	Security

Figure 10.1   NASA KM Framework

Summary and Next Steps

In this chapter we provided you with a robust template for mapping out the Knowledge Management framework you will introduce as part of your strategy and will test in the pilot project that we discuss later. As part of filling in this template, you will need to do some thinking about the information and content management elements of your strategy (Collection and Push, as we described in Chapter 1). Use the following chapter to guide that thinking.

Note

1. NASA Knowledge Management Team, "Strategic Plan for Knowledge Management," April 2, 2002, page 8, accessed July 10, 2014. http://redalternative .wikispaces.com/file/view/Strategic+Plan+for+Knowledge+Management.pdf.

Chapter 11

Information and Content Management

There is a lot of discussion about whether information and content management fit into the Knowledge Management (KM) picture or not. While an arguable point, the fact is that for many organizations this is where they start with KM. They then evolve into more of the traditional KM activities, activities that have a clearer link to organizational learning, e.g. lessons learned, after-action reviews, and communities of practice. Other organizations address both at once.

Documented knowledge is still knowledge; just because it has been captured doesn't make it any less useful, in fact many KM processes are about harvesting knowledge and saving it for reuse. We have a whole chapter (Chapter 18) on the special case of creating a knowledge retention strategy, which looks at retaining knowledge from retiring employees; some of that is done through mentoring and communities of practice, but some of that is done through documentation.

In looking at documented knowledge and its inclusion in your KM strategy it might help you to consider it as an output or by-product of your other KM activities. What are you going to do with those artifacts that are generated through your lessons learned processes and after-action reviews? One of the points in capturing that knowledge is to be able to find and reuse it later on. The finding and reusing has to be part of your strategy; so does encouraging people to go and look for previous experiences rather than jumping in and just starting a project or activity. These are additional activities to consider in your change management plan, for example how to get people to learn before doing, where learning before doing is not only asking other people who have done the activity before, but looking at the various pieces of already captured knowledge and learning from that.

Including information and content management (documented knowledge) in your KM strategy involves the following activities:

- Determining a knowledge repository technology for housing the documented knowledge

- Deciding on an information architecture, i.e. taxonomy and metadata

- Defining documented knowledge lifecycle process

A discussion of what you need to include in your KM strategy about each of these areas follows.

Knowledge Repository Technology—Requirements Analysis

It is critical to ensure that the technology you choose to support your KM strategy is fully aligned with that strategy, as discussed in Chapter 12. The process of determining your requirements for that technology

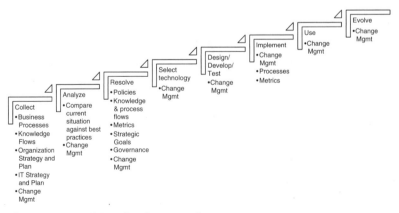

Figure 11.1   KM technology roadmap process

is shown in Figure 11.1. Notice that there are change management activities happening at each step of the process. This ensures buy-in and support, as well as maintaining momentum for the KM program.

The requirements analysis process has eight steps:

1. Collect. This step involves an analysis of the organization's existing KM practices, including current information and knowledge processes or flows, business processes, and organizational culture. Ways to do this are discussed in Chapter 9.

2. Analyze. By reviewing and interpreting the information gathered in the Collect step, you create a framework of processes, knowledge, and information flows, as described in Chapter 12. The information gathered in the Collect step is compared against best practices in order to maximize the value of the recommended activities and technology.

3. Resolve. The analysis from the first two steps is then summarized in a strategic plan document that forms part of your KM implementation plan, as described in Chapter 16.

4. Select software application. Once the strategic plan is created, the organization can take the requirements developed and specified in the Collect–Analyze–Resolve steps and start looking at specific technologies to support and enable the KM strategy.

5. Design/develop/test. Design, develop, and test is a fairly standard set of IT activities. These activities involve users providing input and participation so that the end product meets their needs and requirements and re-work isn't required at a later stage. Each of these activities is iterative and can take weeks or months to complete.

6. Implementation. The Implementation step involves organization staff as much as possible, which helps the organization feel that it is part of the process and will be able to continue with KM on its own once the project is completed and the KM activities are completely implemented. This approach maximizes buy-in and acceptance among staff, helping to ensure the ultimate success of KM within the organization. Implementation sees the development and roll-out of supporting policies

and procedures as well as metrics to measure KM results and activities.

7. Use. At this step of the KM program, the organization is using the KM framework, and the technology within it, in its everyday activities. Governance policies are being executed and monitored by the governance committee and future projects are being planned. Feedback and suggestions for improvements are being collected and implemented where possible and prioritized where they may require budget, longer-term planning, or additional resources not otherwise available as part of regular operational activity.

8. Evolve. In the Evolve step, the feedback and suggestions for improvement received during the Use step are evaluated along with improvements based on new releases in the application from the vendor, as well as changes made necessary by the maturation of the organization. As the organization matures in its use of the technology and KM processes, staff often become capable of using more complex functionality and features, and generally performing more sophisticated tasks with the technology implemented to support their KM activities. This evolution is desired and necessary.

Make Versus Buy

In choosing KM technology there is always the question of do we create our own system, i.e. customized development, or do we buy it off the shelf and configure it to meet our needs?

Make versus buy can be a tactical decision as part of Step 4 of the requirements analysis, described previously. At this point you have to ensure that all factors and requirements have been considered and that a thorough review has been made of the applications that are available in the marketplace. There is a wide variety of applications available for purchase or through the open source community; they can be purchased for installation in the organization's technology environment or purchased for use in a cloud computing environment.

Alternatively, make versus buy can be a strategic decision, driven by your organization's information technology strategy. Many organizations have already decided that, as a strategy, they will never "make" technology, but instead will look for out-of-the-box solutions where support can be outsourced. You should be very clear on the constraints of your organizational IT strategy before you get to this decision point.

Information Architecture

An organization's information architecture is typically comprised of taxonomy and metadata components, which are used in the classification and organization of knowledge and information. Taxonomy is normally thought of as a folder structure or hierarchy, whereas metadata are data concerning a document, such as creator, owner, review date, and archive date. Development of the information architecture usually comes after development of the strategy, but your strategy document should outline how this architecture will be developed.

Development Process

In the development of a taxonomy and metadata, you should determine the organizational needs through questions such as these:

- What are the processes that need to be supported?
- What are the knowledge flows?
- How do people currently think about the information and documented knowledge they use?

These questions and others will be examined and discussed in detail at taxonomy workshops that the KM team will facilitate. The process for the taxonomy and metadata development starts with planning and preparing for the workshops. The number of workshops you'll need and who should participate in them depends on the scope of the taxonomy and metadata that is being developed. It is critical that the taxonomy and metadata align with the processes, knowledge flows, and nomenclature of the organization.

The workshops and alignment with processes, knowledge flows, and organizational terminology result in buy-in and support of the information architecture (taxonomy and metadata) component of the KM project and lead to the completion of the synthesis phase where a final taxonomy is agreed upon and a report generated that captures a summary of the discussions and decisions made in the execution of the workshops.

This is a very brief discussion about the process for developing taxonomy and metadata (information architecture)—there have been whole books and courses written that detail the process of taxonomy development. Here, we highlight the importance of taking the time to be thoughtful and thorough in their development, while leaving the detailed steps and activities for others to describe.

Documented Knowledge Lifecycle Process

A documented knowledge lifecycle process is a process primarily for organizing and storing the documents and other knowledge artifacts that exist within the organization; it considers everything that happens to documented knowledge from creation to archiving and/or deletion.

Like your information architecture, the documented knowledge lifecycle isn't part of your KM strategy per se, however, it is important to recognize that you will need to develop one in order to be successful in organizing your documented knowledge. Otherwise your documented knowledge will become outdated and useless to your organization, which in all likelihood will mean the demise of your KM program. The documented knowledge lifecycle process will be part of the Governance element of your KM framework as covered in Chapter 10.

A documented knowledge lifecycle is depicted in Figure 11.2. It starts with the capture of knowledge or creation of a document. During the Capture/Create stage there are collaboration and workflow activities happening in order to complete the document and approve it before it is published in the Store phase. In the Store phase documents are placed in the approved knowledge repository, with appropriate metadata and security. The repository has the necessary taxonomy and disaster recovery processes in place so that documentation is findable within the system and so that the system is available in the case of an outage.

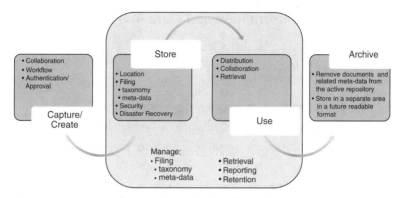

Figure 11.2   Documented knowledge lifecycle

Once the document/artifact is stored, it can be used for reference and information/knowledge purposes by staff. In the repository, the documents are managed, making sure they remain current, and remain accessible when the taxonomy or metadata change. Documentation may be updated while it is housed in the repository. Ideally that means that the owner updates it (getting appropriate approvals, where necessary) and creates a new version rather than a whole new document, although this relies on the repository software to have versioning as one of its features.

Once a document/artifact is no longer useful it should be removed from the repository and archived and/or deleted according to your organization's records retention policy.

In order to manage the repository/repositories, some metadata, reporting, and an escalation path are required. The metadata allow the reporting and include the following tags/flags:

- Owner

- Review date

- Archive date

- Creator

- Review required (this should be a flag for users to indicate that they have found problems with the document)

- Last accessed (this should be system generated)

Example of an Information and Data Architecture

The KM Strategy for Health Canada[1] contains this component on information and data architecture:

> 3.2 Create and enhance data and information models.
>
> Create models with which to structure health data and information. In the case of health information, continue to refine and expand the Health Canada Business Model. Promote the business model as a tool for structuring all departmental information regardless of format and business line. Continue to incorporate the business model into records management processes and the organization of the departmental website.
>
> In the case of health data, continue to support and participate in the CIHI Information Model Group's efforts to create a national health data model to facilitate the sharing of data across jurisdictions and technical platforms. Identify and support existing and proposed Health Canada data models and integrate them into CIHI's emerging national health data model. Identify areas in which the data model could be "drilled down" to enable sharing across databases. Use modeling techniques to map and improve existing business processes.

Summary and Next Steps

Successfully incorporating the information and content management elements of your strategy will require you to pay particular attention to the type of technology you will use for the knowledge repository, the taxonomy and metadata structure that will define your information architecture, and the documented knowledge lifecycle process. This chapter presented methodologies and templates for defining each of these (technology, information architecture, and documented knowledge lifecycle). Once this work has started, you can begin to think about the broader aspect of KM technology selection to complete your framework.

Note

1. Health Canada, "Vision and Strategy for Knowledge Management and IM/IT for Health Canada" (Ottawa: Health Canada, December 1998), www.providersedge.com/docs/km_articles/ Health_Canada's_Vision_and_Strategy_for_KM.pdf.

CHAPTER **12**

Knowledge Management Technology

This chapter is a little different from the others; it takes a deeper look at the technologies that are available to support your Knowledge Management strategy and talks about the process of understanding your requirements and picking the right technology. This is a vital component of your KM strategy, and will comprise a significant portion of your KM strategy document. Understanding the technology requirements and picking the right technology will be critical to your KM success.

As we said in Chapters 5 and 6, aligning KM initiatives with the organization is vital. Many KM initiatives have failed because they focused on the technology and not the organizational need. Not only did the initiative focus on technology but in some instances it focused on the wrong technology, especially in the early days of KM. Because of this focus on technology, KM was assumed to be synonymous with technology, so when the technology failed KM failed too. On the other hand, KM initiatives that focused on the people and process part of the equation and used technology as an enabler succeeded far more often than those that did not. All of this has resulted in the great divide of KM: on one side there is people and process and on the other side there is technology.

In reality, KM is not one or the other, it is not people and process versus technology, it is people, process, *and* technology; all of them together, with governance as a fourth enabler, as described in

Chapter 9. It is only in aligning these four pillars that real value is attained for the organization, and that is what this chapter is about.

This idea of aligning business and information technology can be traced at least to the development of the Information Technology Infrastructure Library (ITIL) in the late 1980s. As IT budgets get bigger and the functionality of the technology increases there has been much more written about the criticality of aligning the organization requirements and IT than in the past. It is increasingly important to ensure that the organization is getting the best value possible from its investment in IT. All too often there is a misalignment of goals and objectives between the organization and IT. Either the technology that IT implements for the organization does not meet the goals and objectives of the organization, or the organization does not understand how to modify their behaviors to best utilize the technology that IT has implemented for their benefit.

There are challenges to aligning the organization and IT. In many organizations IT has an adversarial relationship with the rest of the organization, which makes having a productive relationship around KM technologies and activities difficult. Having someone who is an official liaison between the organization and IT often helps the situation, since that person understands both the operational issues at hand and the IT concerns and IT-specific jargon. An understanding of both is important to ensure that any technology that is implemented enables the KM activities.

The following paragraphs outline the steps in aligning KM technology with the organization.

Understand Organizational Objectives

The first thing to do is to understand the organization's operational objectives. This means understanding the issue that the organization is trying to resolve. For example, is the organization trying to increase sales, are they trying to improve marketing campaign results, are they trying to improve communication, is there a collaboration problem that needs to be corrected? Just what is the problem that is being addressed and how does it align with the overall organizational strategy? Understanding the objective(s) underpins not only the selection of the right kind of technology but also the criteria for success and metrics for the initiative. We discussed this in greater detail in Chapter 6.

Understand User Requirements

Before you can align you need to understand the user requirements from an operational perspective. This means asking users what functionality they currently have in any existing tools that they may be using, and what additional functionality they would like to have. This is not as easy as it may sound, as users may not understand the functionality that is available or even know what they want. It is incumbent upon the person surveying the requirements to know the functionalities that are available and discuss them with the users. In some cases this may involve demonstrating technology options to the users; however, this should be avoided if possible, as showing possible solutions too soon can spell disaster for the project through misaligned user expectations.

Part of understanding user requirements is understanding how people do their work. When do they work, how do they work, who do they work with, what tools do they use, and what expectations do they have about the availability of technology and information? These are all important questions to address when determining your technology requirements.

Requirements do not just mean the software but also mean the hardware requirements; for example, what is the availability level of the technology, where geographically should the technology be located, what network bandwidth and redundancy are required in order to meet user needs? Hardware requirements must also be considered.

In understanding user requirements it is important to identify groups of users based on the types of activities they will be doing using the technology. These groups are sometimes called profiles, or personas. For example, community of practice leaders is one type of user group, profile, or persona. These individuals will expect to be able to create a community, add members, send messages, and complete other administrative and facilitative activities for their community using the technology platform. See Chapter 14 for a discussion of stakeholder groups.

In a high technology company that one of the authors worked with, there were two core user groups: one externally focused and the other internally focused. It turned out they had the same needs. They all:

- Worked "whenever"

- Worked "wherever"

- Needed information quickly

- Needed templates

- Needed the support of other staff—access to their knowledge and experience

- Needed to be able to produce deliverables quickly

- Needed to work individually and with cross-functional and cross-organizational teams

- Worked with partners and other third parties and needed secure methods to share information.

It was the content that changed, not the underlying requirements they had for the technology to support their operational processes.

Embed KM in Processes

Once the strategic and process-driven requirements are understood it is important to determine how KM will be embedded in these processes. Do the processes need to change, does the software need to be configured to accommodate existing processes, what needs to happen in order to enable the operational processes with KM?

For example, one of the authors worked with an organization where the technology supported the externally-focused staff's processes and daily work activities, giving them a place to share documents and collaborate with their global colleagues. Thus the technology supported how and when the staff worked and whom the staff worked with, not requiring the staff to change or stop working the way they had always worked.

Training and Communications

Part of the alignment of KM with operational processes includes the training and communication plan. It is important to train staff in the technology that is selected to support the KM activities. Whether that training takes place in a classroom, or through CBT (computer-based training), or through some other means is up to the implementation team to determine. Training will be different for different organizations and for different groups within an organization. The communication strategy and plan, as discussed in Chapter 13 and Appendix A, has to assess the needs of various stakeholder groups and determine the frequency of the messaging to each group, in order to maximize buy-in and support.

KM Metrics

KM metrics are an important part of ensuring that KM technology is aligned with organizational needs. Understanding what the organization needs to measure helps identify the data that needs to be collected as part of the technology implementation. It is a requirement that the technology be able to collect data and report on it in order to meet organizational needs and objectives.

Senior Management Support

Another component of alignment between IT and the wider organization is ensuring that there is passionate and on-going senior management support for KM. It is only through buy-in at senior levels and a relationship between them and IT management that the KM initiative will be able to get the resources it needs to be successful. When other stakeholders see the management alignment and support, they are more likely to support it themselves.

Cross-functional Participation

Implementing KM technology goes across functions in the organization. As such, it is a necessary part of the project to reach out into the whole organization by creating a virtual workgroup to develop the requirements. While at first glance this may seem cumbersome and time-consuming, the investment in involving all stakeholders in the initial planning stages is critical to the success of the project. Soliciting user requirements from all areas of the organization helps to ensure that nothing is missed; it also helps in change management, communication, implementation, rollout support, ongoing maintenance, improvement, and governance activities. Without this kind of involvement across the organization, KM technology may very well be rolled out, only to be perceived as something that IT or another organizational department is forcing on the rest of the organization. If that's the perception, KM will not be adopted and used, resulting in sub-optimal ROI and productivity improvements.

Having implementation leads from across the organization helps to ensure that as the technology and KM activities are rolled out they align with the users and their processes. This allows for minor modifications in configuration if necessary. As we said previously, this distributed model helps ensure buy-in and support from all stakeholders.

Tied into these previous two points is the need for the KM initiative to have relationships with key KM contacts, users, or champions within the organization. Understanding who these people are and the role that they play is critical to the successful adoption of the KM technology and program as a whole. These people are thought leaders, or gateways to the legions of people in their network that they work with either regularly or occasionally. Having the support of these individuals makes the rollout that much easier.

Technology is a Means to an End

It must be remembered that technology is a means to an end, not the end itself. If stakeholders and operational processes are not involved and considered as part of the process of determining what KM technology to purchase or create, the best software in the world can be rolled out to the organization, but no one will use it.

For example, a company in the environmental sector that one of the authors worked with spent $1 million over 5 years rolling out state-of-the-art document management software to the organization, which employed some 1,200 people in two locations, one office in North America and a second office in Europe. As it turned out the only team to use the soft-ware with any regularity was the document management team located in the North American office, where the document management hardware and software were located; other users were frustrated with not being able to find or access information because the server would go down regularly, and they were in another part of the world that did not have access to an IT support team during their operational hours.

Over the course of nine months, the IT team improved the technology infrastructure by putting in a remote cache server for the European users, to improve responsiveness; and redesigned the user interface, to align it with operational processes and nomenclature. These relatively minor modifications resulted in a 40 percent increase in usage and technology satisfaction and saved them from writing off their $1 million dollar investment and starting over.

Adequate Budget

Another consideration in aligning the organization and IT around the KM technology is that an adequate budget must exist to purchase, develop, maintain, and support the right KM technology.

Users will provide lots of requirements and functionality requests that will make their jobs easier. Not all of this functionality needs to be available at the initial rollout, but the functionality does need to be prioritized and a set of "must-have" functionality must be incorporated into the initial technology release. If that core technology functionality is not present users will rebel against the implementation and will continue to do their jobs the way that they have always done them. The investment in planning, technology selection, and development will have been for nothing if the budget to support and maintain those KM technology activities (planning, selection, and development) is not made available.

Requirements Roadmap Process

The Requirements Roadmap Process provides guidance for how to get from management's commitment for KM technology to the successful implementation of that technology. The successful implementation of

KM technology delivers benefits, functionality, and operational solutions. It follows a process that addresses eight phases of the process: collect, analyze, resolve, select software application, design/develop/ test, implementation, use, and evolve. The process itself is discussed in detail in Chapter 11, but incorporating a requirements definition into your technology alignment activities is critical to your success.

Requirements

During the Collect and Analyze phase of the roadmap process (see Figure 11.1), a list of requirements is discovered and matched to a technology that supports the processes and knowledge flows and meets the requirements of the organization. To do the matching successfully, the KM initiative must understand not only the requirements but the functionality of all of the possible technology platforms that might meet those requirements. Most people have a general idea of what technology would help them do their jobs more efficiently and effectively and many of the technologies have overlapping functionality. This can make the choice both easier and more difficult. Easier because any one of several different types of technologies could be chosen and the requirements of the organization would still be met; more difficult because the overlap in functionality in many technologies makes it harder to pick the optimal technology solution.

Types of KM Technologies

There are many, many types of technologies that address in part or in total some aspect of the KM puzzle. Picking the right one can be a challenge, as can gaining an understanding of what is actually required by the organization. There are numerous criteria to consider and operational process-enablers to understand in order to make the right selection. As described in Chapter 10, you will need:

- Technology to allow people to hold conversations and share knowledge through discussion and through question and answer

- Technology to allow people to easily capture and structure new knowledge, in a variety of contexts

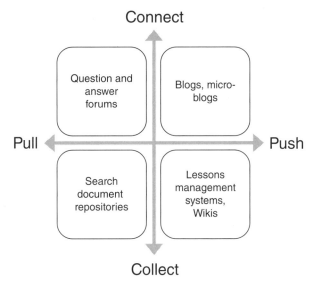

Figure 12.1   Four quadrants of Knowledge Management technology

- Technology to allow synthesis of knowledge from many sources into knowledge assets

- Technology to allow documented knowledge to be searched and retrieved.

Similarly the four quadrants of Figure 1.1 can be used as a template for selecting technology, as shown in Figure 12.1 and discussed in Chapter 1.

The following descriptions provide highlights of use and functionality of the various technology offerings currently in the marketplace. Which (if any) of these you make part of your KM framework depends entirely on the organizational needs, the organizational drivers and the critical knowledge areas that you will already have determined in Chapters 6 and 8.

- Business intelligence applications will report, analyze and present data that has been collected and stored in a data warehouse. The data may be stored elsewhere but a data warehouse provides maximum flexibility and accessibility to the data for ad hoc queries, report writing, and data analysis.

- Customer relationship management or CRM systems manage an organization's interactions with customers, clients, and sales prospects. CRM involves organizing, automating, and synchronizing sales and marketing processes. These systems provide sales and marketing professionals with the information they need to do their jobs, whether it's contact information for clients or prospective clients or the latest datasheet on products or services.

- Contact center software is basically a specialized CRM system used for customer and marketing support. If the organization has clients or customers calling in to a toll-free number, these systems provide the functionality that call-center staff need to answer questions and track the interactions. Call-center software allows for a quick and consistent response to the client/customer.

- Incident management/helpdesk software is another specialized type of CRM system used for technical IT support. It's similar to a contact management system in that it allows for quick and standard responses to questions from IT users. The software supports ITIL (Information Technology Infrastructure Library) processes, a series of best practices for operating an IT department.

- Learning management systems or elearning systems provide the ability to deliver electronic training, mentoring, and performance improvement. Additionally, they support professional trainers and HR staff to deliver training in an organized and systematic way. These systems often allow for the creation of content as well as the testing and tracking of training participants.

- Expertise location systems, sometimes known as Yellow Pages, assist users with finding expertise within an organization or user group. For example, if a professional services organization is using an expertise location system and all staff have set up profiles, everyone can quickly and easily find experts or practitioners in a particular subject area. This is especially key if the staff are new to the organization or the subject matter area and they do not know whom to contact.

- Records Management (RMS) systems enable organizations to maintain their records from creation to ultimate disposal. These systems include functionality that allows records to be classified, stored, secured, archived, and destroyed when necessary. Records Management technologies have comprehensive search functionality, litigation preparedness, military grade security and corresponding certification, as well as the ability to handle both electronic and physical records.

- Component Content Management (CCM) systems address the set of processes and activities that support the collection, managing, and publishing of information in any form or medium. These systems integrate reuse capabilities into whatever application is being used to create the documents; they allow the reuse of text, tables, images, and charts within and across documentation.

- Enterprise Content Management (ECM) systems address the activities surrounding the lifecycle of electronic documents and/ or images of paper documents, i.e. scanned images of paper documents. These technologies support the document management lifecycle, from creation to archive and deletion. They include a search functionality and flexible navigation, as well as customizable taxonomy and metadata. They have check-in and check-out functionality as well as versioning, audit logs, and offline access. Additionally, they will allow for the notification of changes to users who are interested, rating of documents and integration with other applications such as Microsoft Word for the creation of documents and most importantly, they provide security at the document level. ECM systems differ from RMS in that ECM software was developed to make it easier for users with a shared purpose, usually within an organization, to access, manage and collaborate on documents. Access to the documents is enabled by the existence of a library and/or a repository within the system. RMS systems, on the other hand, are concerned with identifying, storing, maintaining and managing data that is used to describe events in an organization's work cycle that are related to statutory, regulatory, fiscal or operational activities within the organization. Record management repositories are generally focused on keeping only what is necessary for a specified length of time.

- Document capture technologies enable information found in a document or image to be captured by scanning the original, no matter what its format. Functionality commonly seen in these technologies allows them to integrate with existing business processes and allows for the flexible viewing of documents/ images. Additionally, these technologies allow the user to add or view notes on documents and to annotate them. As with all the other technologies mentioned, reporting is a key functionality that allows for the administration of the platform and business processes enabled by the technology.

- Search software is technology that allows organizations to find the information they need; it can be enabled on one platform, or across many platforms (known as federated search). Functionality found in search software allows it to personalize search results for particular users or groups and gives users the ability to refine the results using a web interface. Search engines should abide by existing security frameworks so that no user may access a document that they do not have the appropriate security permissions to see. Search technology should also allow the organization to customize the dictionary/thesaurus for words and acronyms that are common to the organization. This makes searching easier and delivers results that are more applicable and relevant to the user's request.

- Semantic Search is technology that allows organizations to find information based on its meaning, rather than the specific words it contains. Semantic search moves beyond alternative words within a dictionary and thesaurus, and a semantic search engine is expected to have embedded knowledge and use it to bring relevant results to the searcher.

- Portal technology provides a framework for the organization to have a single point of access to a variety of information and tools. It may or may not be customizable by the users so that they see information and knowledge that is specific to their needs. Portals integrate with other applications and provide development capabilities that are flexible and extensible; they should be able to easily add users and groups and provide a security model that is easy to setup and maintain. Portals allow for easy, consistent, standardized messaging to go out across the organization. Communities of practice often have their own portals.

- Workflow systems allow a sequence of connected steps to be executed by a user. In the context of KM, the workflows are tied to business processes, documents, and content. Workflow helps to enable the execution of standard processes and knowledge flows across the organization. Functionality commonly found in workflow systems includes drag and drop design, digital signatures and approvals, reporting, integration with other KM technologies, and the ability to narrate a process with instructions. Additionally, workflows should have the ability to override a step and/or appoint a substitute individual when the person normally responsible for the process is on vacation, away sick, or otherwise unavailable.

- eDiscovery is specialized software that aids in discovery for civil litigation. eDiscovery software automates the collection of required documents from various sources, and provides reporting and analytics as well as allowing the user to filter and de-duplicate (remove duplicate records/documents) the identified documents. This type of software should also allow for the annotation and redaction of information within the document, as well as security provisions to control access at the field level. It is critical that hold notices are automated so that documents identified as "on hold" cannot be deleted.

- Blog software allows individuals to create entries of commentary, descriptions of events, or other material such as graphics or video in a diary-type entry. Blogs are typically user-friendly, and support authoring, editing, publishing, widgets, comments, categories/tags, linkbacks, and backlinks; as well as formatting, web syndication and post moderation.

- Microblogging software, e.g. Twitter or Yammer, allows users to broadcast short messages to other users; the content is in the nature of a blog but shorter. Functionality includes the ability to post short messages including URL's and photos.

Microblogging systems often include the ability to create groups and a directory, as well as allowing users to have a profile, send direct messages to other users, and provide appropriate security and access from a mobile device.

- Social networking software is an application or online service that focuses on building and reflecting the social connections among people. Facebook and LinkedIn are well known public domain examples. These applications allow users to create a profile; upload pictures, files, videos, and links; create communities and groups; and send messages to each other while providing appropriate security and integration with mobile devices. The functionality available in these applications is wide and diverse. If you are considering choosing one for the organization to use, it is important to understand what functionality the organization actually needs for effective KM.

- Instant Messaging technology enables real-time, direct, text-based communication between two or more people using computers or mobile devices. Additional features, other than text-based messaging, include such things as file transfers, voice calls, sharing or viewing a desktop, providing user status, and video calling.

- Collaboration technologies allow users to facilitate group work through the use of virtual workspaces and workrooms. Ideally they allow employees, and external partners, to share and create documents. These technologies will often have email capabilities, calendars, and other functionality to facilitate the creation of shared products. A short description of each of the main types of collaboration technologies follows.

  o Collaborative document management technologies have the features of a document management system, plus functionality to aid in creation, for example integration with email and multiple-person real-time editing.

  o Wikis not only support the open, online creation of knowledge assets but also allow the user to upload attachments, control page access, and utilize WYSIWYG (what you see is what you get) editing and versioning.

  o Virtual Meeting software application allows for screen, desktop, or application sharing, so each participant sees the same thing at the same time. It provides the ability to mark up what is being shown in the sharing window, as well as real time audio and recording abilities. There is often the ability to have a text chat that is either public or private, as well as polls and surveys to interact with meeting members.

o   Collaboration suites consist of a whole set of technology within one bundle. Examples of the functionality found in these applications include blogs, calendars, announcements, configurable roles, alerts or subscriptions, instant messaging, polling and surveys, search, and expertise identification.

o   Crowdsourcing applications include mechanisms for collecting input from many people. These can include collaborative mind mapping, survey software, and idea creation and ranking software.

o   Discussion forum technology allows members of a community of practice to raise questions, receive answers, and hold discussions around a topic. This functionality can be found in several collaboration or social media technologies, or it can be developed or purchased as a stand-alone application. Sophisticated versions of discussion forum technology require the user to search existing discussions before raising a new question, allow people to rate the answers they receive, allow questions to be cross posted to multiple forums, and allow questions and discussions to be tagged or categorized with metadata.

- Lesson management systems are designed to facilitate the capture and workflow of lessons learned, making sure that every lesson is carried forward into an action, and into a change in the way the organization works. Lessons are added through a form-based interface, and the lessons management system then tracks and routes the lesson through validation, through assignment of an action, to acceptance and closure of the action. The system will provide reports and statistics covering the effectiveness of lessons management.

- Observation management systems are similar to lessons management systems, but they start by collating observations from many staff around the organization, routing these to an individual or a group who can combine them into a lesson.

Example

As an example of how technology is treated within KM Strategies, the text that follows is taken from the European Centre for Development Policy Management (ECDPM) KM and Communications Strategy[1]. Note that this is more a set of principles governing how they address technology than a selection of individual tools and software.

> 5.5. KMC and ICT innovation
>
> As an organization that is highly dependent on gathering information, communicating and taking part in global exchanges, ECDPM must stay at the forefront of innovations in the field of KMC and ICT and incorporate them in the organization where appropriate. We have been doing so since the Centre's early days and will stick to this priority during this strategic period as well.
>
> Innovations of recent years have increasingly merged KMC approaches with new ICT applications. Advanced technologies and new approaches offer qualitative improvements for networking and reciprocity with policy audiences that were unimaginable when ECDPM was founded. Following this trend, ECDPM has linked its ICT and KMC activities where relevant. The melding of these fields has led to the formulation of the IMAKE project and to other innovations, such as our use of social media and of digital information management tools. We will maintain the KMC–ICT platform, introduced earlier, to review organizational needs and experiences, to formulate strategic advice to management on further innovations, and to guide the Centre in implementing collaborative approaches to knowledge management and policy brokerage.
>
> Our focus on innovation will keep us alert to new technological developments for monitoring and to ways to further improve our news services, knowledge networking and outreach. We are particularly aware of expanded use of mobile devices and location-independent cloud computing

applications. We will incorporate these new approaches where appropriate.

To capitalize on our solid understanding and years of experience in knowledge management and brokerage using new ICT and KMC approaches, we will identify opportunities for advisory services that we can offer to partners and other organizations wanting to take a leap forward in knowledge management and communication. This is an emerging area. We will further explore and assess what additional resources we might need to realize such services.

Summary and Next Steps

KM technology is one of the components of the KM framework you will put in place as a result of your strategy. This is a tricky topic. There are so many technology options to choose from that a disciplined approach is needed if you are to choose wisely and strategically and maximize the return on your investment in KM technology. Make sure your technology selection is based on organizational objectives and user requirements and is supported by training, communication, metrics, and cross functional participation.

Now that you have made a start with technology, it is time to start thinking about the whole issue of change management.

Note

1. European Centre for Development Policy Management "ECDPM's Knowledge Management and Communications Strategy 2012–2016" (Maastricht, The Netherlands: ECDPM, September 2012), accessed May 29, 2014, http://ecdpm. org/wp-content/uploads/2013/09/ECDPM-Knowledge-Management-Commu-nications-Strategy-2012-2016.pdf.

CHAPTER 13

Change Management

The third of the 10 Knowledge Management strategic principles mentioned in Chapter 4 states that an organization must invest in both individual behavior changes and ultimately an organizational culture change if a KM implementation is going to succeed. KM is about changing the way people think. It is about changing personal and organizational priorities. It is about changing the way people treat knowledge. It is a profound shift from the individual to the social collective. These changes must be managed.

Principles of Change Management

Your KM Strategy should utilize the principles and structure behind change management. Those principles are pretty well established, and will not require too much extra research from you. They are based on the work of leadership guru Dr. John Kotter.[1]

- Create a case for change
- Create a "Guiding Coalition"
- Develop a Compelling Vision for Change
- Develop a Communication Plan
- Empower Broad-based Action
- Create (and Communicate) Short Term Wins
- Remove the Barriers to Change
- Embed the Change

Principle: Create a Case for Change

You will need to create a compelling and urgent case for the KM change, linking this back to the organizational drivers and organizational strategy (as discussed in Chapter 6). You need to define this case within the strategy document, as it is part of the rationale for proposing KM and will help those reading the strategy to understand the need for change. The change management plan, which includes the case for change, is separate from the KM Strategy, but the two are inextricably linked and definitely inform each other.

Principle: Create a "Guiding Coalition"

You will need a "guiding coalition," a group of highly placed influential senior leaders to support the change. This is part of the role of the steering team described in Chapter 19. Ensure this team is senior enough to command respect, diverse enough to cover all aspects of the organization, and complete enough that anyone left out cannot block the change.

Principle: Develop a Compelling Vision for Change

You must develop a compelling vision, which serves three functions in change initiatives:

- It clarifies the direction for change

- It motivates staff to take action in the right direction

- It guides decision making.

You have already created a vision as part of the strategy, as described in Chapter 7. Make sure this vision is simple and compelling enough to act as a direction for change.

Principle: Develop a Communication Plan

You must develop a communication plan. While this will follow the strategy, yet not be part of it, your KM strategy should outline the communication principles that you will use. For example:

- You will conduct a communication campaign as part of change management

- You will create a communication plan to coordinate the campaign
- The KM lead will be the focal point for the generation of KM content for all communication channels
- A stakeholder communication chart will be created and used to focus the communications effort (as described in Chapter 14)
- A standard communication pack will be created and used to convey the agreed message to all staff
- Communication with all staff will occur quarterly
- Early demonstrable, quantifiable wins will be sought and publicized as success story case studies, to improve internal positive perception

A template for a communication plan is included as Appendix A.

Principle: Empower Broad-based Action

Empowering broad-based action is about aligning the organization's structure with the goals and objectives of the KM program. Certainly the KM structure should align with the overall organization structure, but it should also align with the needs of the KM program. For example, sometimes the layers of middle management do not completely understand the purpose and objectives of KM and their role in implementing it, so they can second-guess decisions that have been made and create chaos and confusion. Thus it is important that those middle management ranks understand the objectives of the KM program and their role in implementing and supporting KM. Open, honest communication with the people in these roles is key to addressing the needs of this principle.

Principle: Create (and Communicate) Short Term Wins

Once of the principles of KM outlined in Chapter 3 is that KM implementation should contain a piloting stage in which short term wins are created and communicated. Specific advice for Pilot selection is given in Chapter 15; however, the change management component of the piloting stage is discussed here.

In a piloting strategy you take a small part of the organization through the culture change first, in order to:

- demonstrate the value and viability of behavior change to support KM through short term wins and stories describing those wins

- create an "attractor" for the rest of the organization

- test out the KM framework in case any adjustments are needed

Good stories of significant short term wins, told by the people involved, are powerful and help answer the question "What's in it for me?" that is critical in motivating people to change their behaviors. One of the things that works in your favor is that the KM processes used in the pilots encourage changes in behavior, which when done over a period of time lead to culture change. The processes promote openness; people will learn that there is no penalty for openness, sharing, and learning, and that their questions will receive answers. KM processes such as after-action review and retrospect promote reflection, learning, and a performance focus, through discussions on, "What did we set out to achieve?" and "What actually happened?" Community of practice interactions and other knowledge sharing mechanisms promote a sense of interdependence.

Peer assists are a prime example. By giving people space and structure to exchange critical knowledge, and by making it legitimate to ask others for help, you not only create a culture of openness and sharing, you also start to build a sense of community between the project team and the peer assisters. After-action reviews have a similar behavior change effect.

Principle: Remove the Barriers to Change

People don't want to change from their existing behaviors, and you will constantly be working to remove the barriers to change as you move through the rollout of your KM program. Understanding what the barriers are is done through conversations and interviews, observations, and surveys. People will have their own unique reasons for wanting things to stay the same. Part of understanding the barriers and removing them is being able to answer the question, "What's in it for me?" for anyone and everyone who is expected to participate in the KM processes. In some cases having senior management communicate and promote KM can help, but very rarely will it be enough.

Later in the KM implementation, structural barriers can be removed as you introduce new roles, new accountabilities, new governance frameworks, and new models of rewarding and recognizing KM behaviors. By this stage, KM should be "part of the job," and involvement in KM should no longer be optional.

Principle: Embed the Change

It is important to embed the KM processes in the regular organizational and operational processes that people execute. Delivering the KM framework means delivering a set of roles embedded within the organization chart, a set of KM processes embedded within the workflow, and a set of technologies embedded within the IT suite.

Sometimes people think that once this is done, KM is something that "just happens"; they may think that from this point forward everyone will habitually share and reuse each other's knowledge, and that the need for KM professionals, a KM department, or a KM organizational framework will now disappear.

This is not the case. The change program will deliver a changed organization, and that will be an organization with KM not only built into the culture, but also embedded into work practices, roles, technologies, and governance structures. The KM components of this changed organization are what we describe as a KM framework (see Chapter 10), and as with any management framework it needs its own roles and processes to drive it and embed it into the organizational structure, and a small group to monitor and maintain it. If we draw a parallel between KM processes and financial processes, it is obvious why this is true. Just as there is still a need to have finance and accounting departments to monitor, maintain, report on, and oversee the financial management of the organization after the initial financial management processes are in place, the same is true for KM.

The change program is not over once the framework is in place. The implementation team will hand the framework over to a new team that will operate and maintain the KM initiative, but this original team will still need to communicate and educate and remind people of the importance of KM. Without continued change management in the operation and maintenance mode of the embedded framework, an organization can all too easily slip into a pre-KM state, and KM will be declared as another "failed initiative."

Change Management Plan

The purpose of preparing a change management Plan is to establish a strategy and planned approach for managing organizational change as it relates to the KM initiative. The primary objective is to maximize collective benefits for all involved in the change as it relates to KM and minimize the risk of failure of implementing the change.

KM will have an impact on people's daily lives, significantly affecting how people will manage the day-to-day processes of obtaining information that the organization creates. KM provides a structure for managing access to knowledge and streamlining a wide range of processes. A wide-scale change in all areas of the organization will require a structured plan for identifying key champions and stakeholders, managing communications, and analyzing the impact of change on roles and processes throughout the organization.

The organizational change management strategy will focus on three primary areas:

- Organizational Impact Management
- Stakeholder Management
- Communications Management

Organizational Impact Management

Identifying the impact of change on the organization is a key element of an effective change management plan, which will begin in the early stages of the project. The information obtained throughout the requirements-gathering process will provide a key input to organization impact analysis.

The primary goal of organizational impact analysis is to determine which roles and processes will be impacted and to what extent. In many cases, manually supported processes will no longer be required, which will have a significant impact on how people do their jobs on a daily basis. This information will provide key inputs in preparing the communications plan, helping users and stakeholders understand how their roles will change and how to find new ways to perform their jobs more effectively.

Organizational impact analysis focuses on the following areas:

- Identifying as-is and to-be processes
- Determining process redundancies and efficiencies
- Determining user and stakeholder impact and the extent of the impact
- Identifying areas for improved decision making through centralized information

Stakeholder and Sponsor Management

Stakeholder management identifies individuals or groups affected by and capable of influencing the change management process. These individuals or groups have a direct interest in or will be impacted by the KM initiative.

Management of stakeholders and stakeholder issues is necessary to identify the range of interests that need to be taken into consideration in planning change and to develop the vision and change process in a way that generates the greatest support.

As the stakeholders (or key users) are identified for participation and engaged in the program, the KM Program Manager will develop and refine change management strategies including:

- Identifying stakeholder roles in the change process
- Identifying stakeholders reactions to change and its effects on the program
- Gaining a more complete understanding of political barriers to implementation
- Identifying key input for communication strategy

Key stakeholders will be involved and actively participate in the KM program from the start, in order to provide a sense of ownership in the process and ensure their needs and concerns are being met.

The process of organizational change management can include a variety of key stakeholders, and can be filled by either individuals or groups at various times during the program. A list of stakeholder roles in change management is provided in the following paragraphs, and there is a discussion of other stakeholder roles and responsibilities in Chapter 14.

KM Sponsor. This is the key internal person responsible for initiating communications and coordinating the change process. The Program Sponsor is also responsible for setting the direction for the program and influencing people to follow in that direction.

KM Champion. This is the key person responsible for driving change in their respective organizational area by building and sustaining strong enthusiasms about the change. This often includes reminding everyone in their areas why the change is occurring, as well as communicating the benefits that will come as a result of the KM implementation.

KM Functional Lead(s). This is the key person who will serve a similar role as the Program Sponsor and Program Champion in their respective organizational areas. This will include initiating change and guiding their own development and productivity as well as that of other individuals and groups they interact with.

Communication: Planning and Management

The ability of the KM Program to successfully achieve its vision is largely dependent on the effective delivery of targeted communications to the organization. Users and stakeholders alike will need to have a key understanding of why the KM Program is being undertaken, how their jobs will be impacted, and what the benefits are from implementing the KM Program.

Stakeholder and Organizational Impact Management activities will provide key input in determining communications requirements and will be used to help develop an effective communication strategy and plan, which includes:

- Identification of specific audiences for targeted communication (groups, business users, etc.)

- Identification of barriers and enablers to communication
- Identification of the most effective communication vehicles

Communications planning will encompass stakeholder and the organizational community at-large and will consist of the following steps:

1. Articulate the KM Program Purpose
2. Identify Key Stakeholders (Target Audience)
3. Determine Communication Objectives
4. Articulate Key Messages
5. Identify Appropriate Communication Channels
6. Determine the Communications Frequency and Timeline
7. Communicate the Key Messages

1. Articulate the KM Program Purpose

The goal of articulating the KM Program's purpose is to provide an understanding of why the program is being undertaken and what benefits the organization will gain from the program. Specific objectives include:

- Help all audiences understand their roles in and the value of the program
- Create understanding of the programs among employees so they are willing and able to make the changes
- Define a communications approach appropriate for each of the targeted audiences
- Ensure audiences are aware and ready for the change

2. Identify Key Stakeholders (Target Audience)

The stakeholder groups represent key business areas or groups of individuals with an interest in or impact on the program, many of whom were involved in the requirements gathering focus groups. The communications plan will identify these groups and outline the types of communications best suited to each. See Chapter 14 for more details.

3. Determine Communication Objectives

The goal of determining the communication objectives is to identify what messages need to be communicated to each stakeholder group. Specific objectives include:

- Ensuring stakeholders are able to manage changes and make appropriate decisions

- Adhering to a consistent change communication approach and message

- Ensuring stakeholders understand the value of KM (to themselves, and to the business)

- Ensuring end users are ready for the change

- Timely and effective communication of relevant information to individual stakeholder groups

4. Articulate Key Messages

Part of the success of the program will depend on outlining the key messages to convey to each stakeholder group. This includes messages regarding the value of the program to employees, what stakeholders are expected to do, and the expected outcome for the organization.

5. Identify Appropriate Communication Channels

The communication channels determine how you will communicate with the various stakeholder groups and users, keeping in mind limitations such as access to internal systems or geographical location.

6. Determine the Communications Frequency and Timeline

Your communications frequency and timeline is a schedule you will create for sharing information; it will specify key communication items and provide dates for their distribution to appropriate stakeholders and users.

7. Communicate the Key Messages

Once you have successfully completed the previous steps, it is critical that you actually execute the plan and communicate the key messages. These messages will need to be repeated regularly by various leaders and KM program stakeholders and participants, and may need to be adjusted based on results and feedback, but once you have done all of the work to outline these activities, it is now a matter of following through and sharing the messages with the organization.

Training: Planning and Management

Training stakeholders and users in KM processes, and in the delivery of their KM accountabilities, will be critical to the success of KM adoption. The training plan will assess the fundamental differences between the as-is and to-be processes as identified in the KM Strategic Plan and target the training according to the needs of each target audience.

Additionally, training strategies will define not only how the users are to be trained but what they will be trained on. This includes plans for training local users, as well as remote users who may not have access to instructor-led training approaches.

The original training plan details the program training required for the initial phase. It should be noted that training will need to continue as new people are on-boarded, as staff change roles and as new activities and applications are rolled out as part of the overall KM framework. For these reasons, the training plan will need to be periodically updated to reflect changes in both the KM program and organizational requirements.

Summary and Next Steps

Change management is a key component and contributor to the success of the KM program. People in all roles and with all types of responsibilities need to understand what is in it for them in order to willingly change their behaviors. Understanding their behaviors and the best way to communicate with each and every one of them is crucial in order to successfully implement the entire KM program and to ensure that it meets their needs and expectations. Part of change management will be the identification of key stakeholders, and this is something we cover in the following chapter.

Note

1. Kotter International, "The 8-Step Process for Leading Change," accessed May 29, 2014, http://www.kotterinternational.com/our-principles/changesteps/changesteps.

CHAPTER 14

Stakeholders

So far we have been addressing strategy from the point of view of "what." What knowledge, what organizational focus, what framework, and so on. However, there is another point of view on strategy, and that is the "who" point of view.

Implementing Knowledge Management (KM) is a change process, as we discussed in Chapter 13, and managing change involves managing stakeholders.

Your KM strategy document should identify these stakeholders, and their degree of interest and influence, and prioritize how you will approach them.

Stakeholder Influence Models

A useful plot for mapping out your stakeholders is shown as Figure 14.1, and this is a good place to start. On this plot you map each stakeholder against his level of influence and level of interest. This mapping divides stakeholders into four stakeholder groupings.

- The high interest, high influence grouping are the key stakeholders, who require involvement and input into the strategy, and who have a high interest in the KM implementation.

- The low interest, high influence grouping are also key stakeholders, and will need to be canvassed and communicated with during the program. They will not have input to the strategy.

- The high interest, low influence grouping are the knowledge workers in the organization who will be affected by the pilot projects.

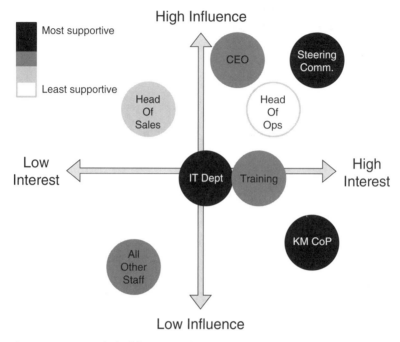

Figure 14.1   Stakeholder groupings

- The low interest, low influence grouping probably represent the majority of non-managerial staff. These stakeholders need to be kept informed of the progress of the KM implementation, and of the role that they will play in the final KM framework.

You can map your stakeholders on this plot, and also color-code them by their degree of support. In Figure 14.1, for example, you can see a key stakeholder in the high interest, high influence segment who is coded white, due to his lack of support. You will have to focus a lot of attention on stakeholders like this, lest they derail the KM project.

Who Are the Key Stakeholders?

In addition to the stakeholders discussed in Chapter 13, there are some organizational stakeholders to whom you must pay attention. These are:

- The senior management team
- The CEO

- Prominent senior skeptics
- Key department heads
- The sponsors of pilot projects
- The knowledge workers in the organization
- The KM community of practice
- External bodies

We discuss each of these in the following sections.

The Senior Management Team

The members of the senior management team are perhaps your most important stakeholders. In order to embed KM in the business, changes to the business will eventually need to be made and they will come from that team. You may have to change the incentives policy, perhaps removing the "factory of the year" award that drives so much internal competition. You may need to change accountabilities within the organization, add additional processes to the business management system, and/or add new technology to the IT portfolio. For all of these you will need support at the highest level. The best way to ensure this support is to request a high-level steering team to oversee your KM project, including the CIO, the head of HR, the head of projects, the head of operations, etc. You can request that these senior managers help steer your program, and in return for this oversight you may receive their support. This steering committee will also be very influential in driving the required KM behavior and ultimate culture change, as described in Chapter 13.

The CEO

Of course the chief executive is a key sponsor, but many chief executives are happy to delegate oversight of the KM program, as long as there is a good steering committee in place. The CEO has massive influence, but probably only mild interest, and may not be an active supporter until you have demonstrated the extent of the value that KM can bring to the organization.

Prominent Senior Skeptics

The prominent doubters, or the high-level skeptics, are important stakeholders, even though they may not recognize themselves as such. It is worth engaging these people early, listening to their concerns and worries, and learning what might convince them to support your KM program. We worked with a KM team in a television broadcasting company, where the staff of one particular division was highly skeptical of the value of KM. The team decided to ignore this division, and work with people who were more supportive. However, at the learning review at the two-year mark, the team recognized that this decision was a mistake. It would have been better to have worked more closely with the skeptics, and either to have asked them to suspend judgment until the results came in, or to have done enough work early on to gain their support. There are few culture change agents as powerful as a prominent skeptic who becomes an ardent supporter.

If skeptical individuals are not too influential, however, you may choose to ignore them. In a technology company one of the authors worked with, the KM program team decided to leave the quality team on the sidelines and work with teams that were interested in participating in the KM team's activities. Eighteen months later the quality team was under pressure to cut their budget and decided to participate in the KM team's activities after all, finally becoming one of the KM team's biggest supporters and proponents. It was widely believed that if the quality team had been forced to participate at the beginning they would have been the KM team's biggest detractors.

Key Department Heads

There are certain key departments in the organization where there is an inherent degree of overlap with KM. If we think of KM as involving the four enablers (people, process, technology, and governance), then each of these enablers will intersect with another organizational body, as shown in Figure 14.2.

- The people aspect is linked to HR and to training, as new roles may need to be put in place, new career ladders established, and new recognition schemes introduced

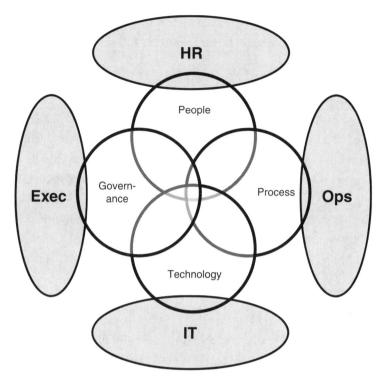

Figure 14.2   Key departments for KM

- The technology aspect is linked to IT, as new software applications, systems and (sometimes) hardware need to be in place

- The process aspect needs to be linked to operations, as new processes have to be embedded into the operational workflow

- The governance aspect needs to be linked to executive management, as their support, involvement, and drive is vital.

The heads of each of these departments are important stakeholders, and should be on your steering committee.

The Sponsors of Pilot Projects

We will talk about pilot projects in Chapter 15, and part of the selection criteria for pilots is to find a supportive sponsor. These people will have massive influence on the success of your KM strategy; good piloting results will be a massive boost to moving KM forward.

The KM Community of Practice

There will be KM enthusiasts in your organization, the KM community of practice. They see the value in KM, they "catch the vision," they are enthusiastic and they are very easy and rewarding to work with. Given their interest, they can be influential at middle and lower levels in the organization. They are an important stakeholder grouping and fun to work with, with endless enthusiasm and energy. However, unless your KM strategy extends beyond the enthusiasts, you risk ending up "preaching to the choir." The KM fans will create a KM bubble, and if you don't move beyond the enthusiasts you won't penetrate the rest of the organization.

External Bodies

For many organizations involved in the creation and distribution of knowledge, some the main stakeholders may actually be external to the organization. The Republic of Kenya Climate Change KM Strategy[1], for example, identifies the following external stakeholders, who will be the end-users of the knowledge-based documents:

- The general public
- Policy makers and implementers
- Research and academic institutions
- Educational institutions
- Civil society organizations
- Private sector
- Development partners
- The media

If your KM Strategy involves creation of material for external users, you too might have a large list of external stakeholders.

How to Influence the Stakeholders

The best and the simplest way to influence the stakeholders is to listen to them. KM will only add value if it solves problems, so listen particularly carefully to the stakeholders in operational units who are potential pilot sponsors. Identify what their knowledge problems might be, and ensure your KM Strategy helps address these problems. Your stakeholders need to see not only that KM delivers value to the organization, but also that it delivers value to them personally, and to their departments. So determine:

- Their business challenges

- Their "hot issues"

- The knowledge they need to help them with these issues and challenges

- How KM could give them access to this knowledge

Next, find some stories or case studies where other people in similar situations have been able to use KM not only to deliver business results, but also to make their own lives easier. Even better, work out a way in which KM could help address the problem through an early stage pilot. This is what we call the "Principle of Local Value." People will support a new initiative, provided they see it as having tangible value in the local setting. Help them see the local value.

We mentioned in Chapter 8 the example of the Mars KM strategy, where KM was seen as "removing the thorn from the lion's paw." They spoke with the senior staff, found what their biggest knowledge issues were, and addressed these one by one, gaining support and endorsement from the senior stakeholders as a result. The biggest decisions are made at the highest level, and there the need for knowledge may be greatest and the application of knowledge can yield the best return. That's where some of the thorniest issues can be resolved through the application of KM, and where you can gain some of your most powerful supporters.

Hearing from the Knowledge Workers

In order to get information from the large numbers of knowledge workers, you have to give them the means to communicate with you, and then you need to really listen to what they are telling you.

A knowledge manager we worked with asked the team leaders in his organization, "What does your team want from the KM project?" That's a very good question, and it allows you to understand some of the issues KM must address. Bear in mind, however, the people that you are asking will probably have a superficial understanding of KM, and they don't know what they don't know. Don't be restricted by their answers.

Here are the answers that the knowledge manager received from his team leaders, expressed as a "wish list."

- A central place to be able to store and find key information and knowledge in an organized and easily accessible way

- A clear place to be able to show new staff where key information is kept, as part of their orientation

- For each team to have a "learning conscience" person to connect with

- For service/support teams, the information they need to be integrated with the learning of the teams they support

- When people leave, or are absent for periods, their knowledge be captured by exit interview for others to use

- Capturing lessons learned to avoid "reinventing the wheel"

- A way to know who knows what in the organization

- More collaboration and learning between teams

- Increase in interpersonal connectivity and awareness in the organization

- Clarify the tools and techniques of KM

- A process for managing/coordinating external key relationships

- Clarity about how to transmit organizational values

- To allow for feedback into strategy and planning, a process for a team to take time out to reflect and evaluate their work

- To capture what people come back from long term assignments overseas have learned

- To help plan job moves within the organization, an increased awareness of what other roles are like

- Updated and clear procedures to follow

- Information on why teams are deviating from budgeted plans

You may have noticed that many of the answers are about finding content, not losing knowledge, and about "who knows whom" and general connectivity. There are few if any answers that talk about organizational benefits, so it is critical to be able to extrapolate what the knowledge workers have said and translate it to organizational benefits. Just because knowledge workers don't respond by tying their issues into organizational or strategic terms, doesn't mean the linkage isn't there. Knowledge workers provide critical insight into how KM will help solve their problems, and if their problems are solved, the organization will benefit.

Summary and Next Steps

Change management is a key part of implementing KM, and stakeholder management is a key part of change management. Identify the important stakeholders, and use one of the templates we offer in this chapter to determine how best to manage them. Once this mapping is complete, you can move on to the next piece of work: determining a small set of KM pilot projects.

Note

1. Republic of Kenya, "Climate Change Action Plan 2013-2017 - Subcomponent 7: Knowledge Management and Capacity Development" (Nairobi: Ministry of Environment and Natural Resources, November 2012), www.kccap.info/index. php?option=com_phocadownload&view=category&id=42.

CHAPTER 15

Pilot Projects

One of the 10 principles listed in Chapter 4 is that a KM implementation should include a piloting stage, and running one or more Knowledge Management pilot projects is an important step in the implementation process. A pilot project is a phase in which you apply all of the KM framework to a part of the business, in order to road test the framework prior to rolling it out across the organization. Your strategy should not just explain the need for pilots, but also present a short list of potential pilot projects.

About Pilots

For the purposes of this chapter and our approach to KM strategy and implementation, we differentiate between a pilot of the whole framework and a test of one process, technology or role. Some organizations refer to them both as pilots, but there is an important difference between piloting the whole framework versus piloting one single component. Because KM works as a system, and delivers the best results when the whole system is applied, then you haven't truly tested it, nor proven its value, until you pilot the whole framework.

A pilot is therefore not something like "piloting a Wiki," or "piloting a community of practice," but the pilot of the entire KM framework applied to an organization problem; for example "improving the bidding process through KM," or "increasing new product sales through KM." Piloting the whole framework provides visibility into the end-to-end processes from knowledge creation to knowledge reuse and can help identify any full-process issues, whereas pilots of part of the framework may miss these issues.

If we take the view of pilot projects as being a test of the whole KM framework, there are four things that the pilot projects should deliver.

- The first few pilot projects will be "proof of value" projects, and the organization will be watching them closely to see if they work, and in particular to see whether KM delivers value in an individual context. Until that point, you will meet many people who say "KM sounds fine, and I can understand how it worked at Ford, or Shell, or NASA, but our organization is different." A successful pilot project will demonstrate to these people that KM can indeed deliver value in your business.

- A successful pilot project will deliver a lot of information about how KM works in your business, and how KM can be implemented in your culture.

- A successful pilot will deliver monetary value to the organization, and so is worth doing in its own right.

- Finally, you should be able to get some good material from the pilot project to support your marketing and change management plans, such as stories, user endorsements, quotes, and videos. Such material will be indispensable for the roll-out phase, and will be crucial to your change management efforts, as explained in Chapter 13.

Selecting Pilot Projects

A pilot project addresses organizational "pain points," where better management of knowledge will help solve the problem and alleviate the pain. Examples of these pain points include:

- Operationally critical activity that is new to the organization, and where the firm needs to learn rapidly. KM can help by putting learning systems in place or, if the activity is new to only one part of the organization, transferring learning from where it has been used before.

- Operationally critical activity that is carried out in several locations, and where performance level varies. KM provides a framework for the exchange of knowledge from the good performers in order to improve the poor performers.

- Repetitive activity, particularly high-cost activity, where KM can provide a learning framework to drive continuous improvement and accelerate the learning curve.

- Where an area of the organization is stuck due to lack of knowledge, KM can help develop the knowledge needed to get it unstuck.

- Where a part of the organization is suffering due to the retirement of staff or high staff turnover, KM can help retain knowledge within the organization.

Some of these pain points may well be the same as some of the areas you identified when making the case for Knowledge Management, as discussed in Chapter 3.

A pilot will generally address a practice area; one that could be relevant to many projects, teams, and divisions rather than covering a single project or team. Some of the good pilots we have worked with in the past include:

- Maintenance shutdowns and restarts in refineries
- Developing "route to market" for a new product
- Retail site construction in Europe
- Entering Far Eastern markets
- Marketing pet food in emerging nations
- Winning government contracts
- Reducing the cost of poor-quality products/services
- Business downsizing
- Mergers and acquisitions
- Underground mining techniques.

How to Find Candidate Pilot Projects

In order to find candidate pilot projects for your KM strategy, you need to have a series of conversations at a high level in the organization.

You need to talk with senior managers, project leaders, divisional leaders and heads of departments, in order to find the pain points that KM might address within their project, department, or division. Tell them a few stories about KM in other organizations, give them some examples of where KM has added value, and ask some of the following questions.

- What are the things that you wish you knew, in order to solve your most pressing organizational problems?

- What are the knowledge intensive parts of your organization, and which are the ones where better management of knowledge would help you?

- If teams and managers in your part of the organization had perfect access to the knowledge from within the organization, what problems might be solved?

- What would it be worth to you and the organization if these problems were to be solved?

It is good to get this final question answered in monetary terms, even if it is only in an order of magnitude sense, for example "it would be worth millions," or "it would be worth tens of millions."

Do a lot of listening. You should not be putting ideas into people's heads. You should be listening to their problems and helping them understand which of those problems could be solved or alleviated by a KM pilot. Once you've had several of these conversations, you should have a substantial list of potential pilot areas. Focus on the pilots which each organizational area has identified as producing the most savings.

Make Sure You Don't Miss the High-Level Pilots

Many senior managers assume KM is "something my juniors need." They therefore often propose pilot projects that address routine tasks at lower levels in the organization. They might set up a KM program to improve call center response for instance, or to improve shift handover, or to improve productivity on the assembly line. As we explained in Chapter 4, while solving these problems can be valuable, this misses the bigger point.

KM can be of value at all levels. After all, knowledge supports decisions, and decisions are made at all levels, but some of the most valuable and risky decisions are made at senior levels. So look for and propose pilots at senior levels to support the big decisions and at the same time to win over some senior stakeholders. Here are some examples from past KM implementations:

- KM to support mergers and acquisitions. This is a massive high-level task, which requires big decisions. Learning from past mergers can materially improve future mergers. We were engaged by one organization to help them develop standard practices in mergers, acquisitions, integrations and divestments, which involved our working with the in-house KM team to capture knowledge from the firm's chief attorney and several of the other C-level executives.

- KM to support new business. Companies may open new offices or start doing business in different countries. With the right knowledge, such a start-up can be quick and effective; without the right knowledge it may hit snags, be delayed, or fail to deliver the required business results. We have seen some very effective pilots in this area.

- Knowledge of leadership. This is a massive issue! One company does a regular staff survey to measure morale, and used KM tools and techniques to gather insights from the managers of high-morale teams to help develop other leaders in the organization. Another collected and published knowledge of leading winning sales teams, and used this as guidance for other sales team leaders.

Delivering a high-level KM pilot has three immediate benefits:

- It delivers significant value to the organization

- It engages senior managers and helps them understand the value KM can bring

- It gets senior managers on your side by solving their problems for them. These people are often some of the key stakeholders, as described in Chapter 14

To reiterate, KM is needed at all levels, and the sooner you involve the senior managers, the faster and smoother your implementation will be.

Grading and Selecting Pilots

Once you have created a reasonable list of pilots, you need a selection process to hone in on the small number that you will then consider. Generally this will involve ranking the possible pilots against a set of criteria. You can do this yourself, or you can gather your steering team together for a ranking workshop.

We recommend that you use four areas to rank the projects:

- Organization Support
- Measurability
- Scalability
- Feasibility

Organization Support

Your pilot needs good support from the organization. The people you choose to pilot have to be enthusiastic. The manager of the pilot organizational unit must be a supporter of KM, and must be willing to devote resources to the pilot, including assigning an individual who will act as pilot project leader, with support from the KM team. Potentially your pilot project will depend on three key individuals: the organization sponsor (usually the manager of the organizational unit, who will act as customer and will also validate any benefits), the pilot project leader, and the KM expert.

Measurability

Part of the purpose of the pilot is to demonstrate real, measurable value. The results have to be clear enough and measurable enough to provide evidence that KM delivers on its promise. The pilot should address a simple business metric, one where you already have a baseline, and it should be able to deliver improvements above the baseline within the required time frame. There is no point in embarking on a six-month pilot, for example, if you're not going to see the results for 2 years, as this will be too late to use the pilot results as success stories during your roll-out campaign. The pilots that deliver results most quickly are those based on "knowledge pull," such as "learning before" activities that bring knowledge in at the start of the project. That is because the knowledge can be used and applied immediately.

Scalability

The ideal pilot project is one that can be scaled. For example, you may capture knowledge in one part of the organization which can be used elsewhere once the pilot is over. Maybe you are seeking knowledge about new country entry in order to help the start-up business in Japan, which can then be applied to the start-up in Malaysia. This is an example of a scalable pilot, and scalability should be one of your selection criteria.

Feasibility

The pilot needs to be feasible. It needs to be realistic and practical. Do not choose an issue which is too big or too risky to solve in the required time frame. It is better to choose something smaller and simpler which will deliver small but clear benefits. One of our clients attempted to pilot KM on their biggest and most complex project, which was already running into severe issues of timing, quality, and cost overrun. This was an impossible task, and KM had little effect. Instead of going for large and risky projects, prioritize those projects which you believe you can succeed with using the available resources.

Presenting the Pilots within the Strategy

Create a ranking spreadsheet, using the criteria mentioned previously, and use this to select the highest ranking five or six pilots. Present these five or six pilots within the strategy document for review by your steering team and senior sponsors. Write a short paragraph about each pilot, explaining the business problem, giving the name of the sponsor, and describing the core operational metric which KM will address.

Example

The Agency for Clinical Innovation in New South Wales, Australia identifies the following pilot in their KM strategy:[i]

It is recommended the ACI chooses one or two networks to trial/pilot some knowledge activities/initiatives, and enhance the sharing of information through these networks. After-action reviews and lessons learned can be documented and shared more broadly to identify aspects that work well or could be amended or improved and enhance communications across and between networks.

Summary and Next Steps

Piloting is a vital step within your KM strategy, allowing you to test and validate your KM framework prior to rolling it out across the organization. Select pilots that address a pain point, and have organizational support, measurability, scalability, and feasibility. Don't ignore the pilots at senior management level as these can be the most valuable.

Once you have defined a good set of pilots—selected to succeed—you can move on to the next step, finalizing the business case and determining the return on investment (ROI).

Note

1. Agency for Clinical Innovation, "Knowledge Management: An ACI Approach" (Chatswood, NSW, Australia: Agency for Clinical Innovation, 2013), page 18, accessed July 10, 2014. http://www.aci.health.nsw.gov.au/__data/assets/pdf_file/0019/203680/ACI-Knowledge-Management-Approach2013.pdf.

CHAPTER 16

Making the Business Case and Determining ROI

At the point at which you are writing the strategy document, it will not be possible to calculate and define an accurate Return on Investment (ROI) for Knowledge Management. You are not yet proposing to roll out KM across the whole organization; you are merely asking for the funding to run some pilot projects. The results of the pilot projects should then allow you to make a proper business case supported by an ROI figure.

You have already made the business case for a strategy; we showed you how to do this in Chapter 3. If there is still suspicion or concern in your organization about the value of doing KM, then you may choose to add an outline business case and ROI in your strategy document in order to justify investment in piloting. If you haven't picked up any signals about concern over value, then don't include the business case, as it may raise more questions than it answers.

The main message you need to get across in the outline business case is the scale of the value, or the "size of the prize" that KM might deliver in the long term.

Estimating the Size of the Prize

Estimating the size of the prize/reward/payback from KM is a tricky step, but there are a few ways to address this.

First, you will have a series of benefit estimates from your discussions about potential pilot areas, and you can use these as an order of magnitude estimate. For example, if one operational division believes it would be worth tens of millions of dollars to have better access to knowledge, and there are 10 operational divisions, then you can assert that the scale of the prize is hundreds of millions.

Second, you can gather some baseline statistics, in areas such as the following:

Increasing Market Share—Win Ratio

Improved bid success rate is a commonly applied focus for KM in organizations that win work through competitive bidding. To make an estimate of how much value KM can bring, you need to know your average bid success rate as well as the bid success rate of your best bid team. If all the bid teams could reproduce the success of the best team, work out the ballpark value of that added business. Next make a plausible estimate of how close you could get to that success rate if you could transfer the crucial knowledge from the best team to the other teams. It's unlikely that KM alone will bring each team up to the standard of the best, but maybe you can get them 20 percent of the way there.

The potential value of the KM program is equal to the value multiplied by the effectiveness. For example if the average bid success rate is 30 percent while the best team delivers 50 percent, you might calculate that it was worth $50 million to bring everyone up to the level of the best, but that transferring knowledge through KM could close the gap by 20 percent. In this case the expected return from KM is 20 percent of $50 million, or $10 million.

Now you could argue that 20 percent improvement is quite a soft target. Why not aim for 50 percent? Why not aim for 100 percent? And yes, maybe it is a soft target, but experience of KM business cases has shown us that the best policy is to under-promise and over-deliver.

Increasing Market Share—Improving Time to Market

The faster you can get your new product or offer into the market the more likely you are to be the dominant player in that market, and to capture the dominant market share. This principle is frequently referred to as the first mover advantage. To estimate the value that

KM might deliver in this area, you again need to get some baseline data. What is your best historical time to market? What is the average time? If you could capture the knowledge from the best projects, by what extent might you improve that average? If you improved time to market, what additional market share would you capture, and what would that additional business be worth? It is important, in every case, that credible people in the business estimate these figures, based on good historical data. Then again you need to estimate how effective KM could be in delivering that accelerated time to market. In this case, the equation is not a simple one, as there will not be a linear relation between the accelerated time to market and the increased market share.

Increasing Market Share — New Markets

New market entry is a similar case to the time-to-market example. If you can enter a new market quickly and efficiently through applying the knowledge from the past, you can potentially gain first mover advantage and capture a larger market share. We worked with one company in a knowledge exchange focused on new market entry in the Far East, and at the end of the exercise, estimated that we had exchanged knowledge that would improve the ROI by $4.8 to $6.5 million.

Another of our clients compared market penetration in a number of new markets, and estimated the value that would be delivered if each new market showed the same level of penetration as the best. This value figure is worth billions, and is the prize that their KM program is accessing through constructing community-based task forces to share knowledge between marketing teams in existing and emerging markets.

Increasing Margins — Global Harmonization of Best Practices

Imagine you are working in a business with multiple operating or manufacturing sites. Operations cost, and manufacturing cost, will vary from site to site. KM gives you the opportunity to reduce these costs, by transferring lessons learned and best practices from low cost sites, to improve the performance of high cost sites.

In order to make a business case for your KM intervention, you need:

- A good set of benchmark data on current operational costs, broken down as far as possible into the different factors

- An estimate of how effective KM could be in normalizing those costs

- A desire across the business to improve. The high cost sites need to want to improve. The low cost sites need to want to help them.

For example, one of our clients looked at one of their major cost elements, water usage, and benchmarked it around their global sites. They set a target of top quartile, and assumed that KM, at the very least, would move each site 10 percent of the way towards this top quartile target. Even this modest estimate of improvement was worth $7 million annually to the organization, which would more than cover the costs of the community of practice needed to exchange the knowledge.

Increasing Margins—Optimizing the Learning Curve

Any new plant, or new operation within a plant, will experience a learning curve. Initially it will run inefficiently, but as the expertise of the team improves and methods of working are perfected, a maximum efficiency will be reached. Production time will decrease; production cost will decrease. You could assert that the only thing the team has at the foot of the curve, which it did not have at the top, is knowledge; knowledge of how to configure and run the plant at maximum efficiency. All of the area under the curve represents the cost spent in acquiring knowledge. KM can accelerate the learning, and by allowing more efficient and effective learning can reduce these costs.

While the learning curve effect is seen in all repetitive operations such as installing double glazing, building small retail shops, or repairing traffic lights, the value that can be delivered from learning faster is greatest for high-cost operations such as drilling oil wells, building airports, or opening factories. Oil companies drill a series of wells on each oil field and the cost of these wells inevitably comes down over time. Comprehensive records of these costs are kept, allowing a historical database of learning curves to be developed. These show the difference in value between teams that learn quickly, using KM tools and techniques, and those that do not. See what records you have that demonstrate learning curves, find the examples of fastest learning, and calculate the value that would be delivered if all programs learned just as quickly.

Increasing Margins—Risk Reduction

Risk is a source of potential cost or lost revenue. Whether it is the risk of losing a client, the risk of making a repeat mistake, the risk of shutting down an operation, or the risk of producing a substandard product, all risks carry cost. Knowledge can reduce risk. If you know what to do, then you can avoid, or manage, those risks. If you are trying to make a business case for KM through risk reduction, you need to estimate:

- The financial impact of the risk
- The current likelihood of the risk
- The degree by which the likelihood will be reduced by your planned KM intervention

Ask people from the organization to estimate the first and second of these, while you may need to come up with the third estimate.

Very often, when KM supports risk reduction, the magnitude of the risk makes the business case for approving the KM program obvious. One of our clients, who provided service to a global customer base, saw the potential value in KM when the same error in service delivery was picked up by the same global customer in three separate sites. They realized that if this were to happen a fourth time they would lose that customer, with a massive impact on revenue. As a result they invested in building a community of practice, so that errors could be reported and solutions exchanged on a real-time basis.

Increasing Margins—Decreasing Overhead

One common method for justifying investment in KM is to estimate the increase in productivity KM will give you through reducing the time you spend seeking knowledge. Hughes Space and Communications Group took this approach in the 1990s, when they found that their employees were spending 40 percent of their time performing knowledge work that others had done. If employees could find the knowledge they needed, rather than needing to reinvent it, they could free up personal productivity. Imagine the potential benefit to your organization if you could provide your best thinkers, most efficient workers, and most innovative staff with more time for innovative thinking. Imagine what they could do to your competitive position in the marketplace.

In companies that provide time-written billed services to clients, such as lawyers or consultants, a decrease in overhead may be one of the few ways that KM can increase margin. One of the main consulting companies focused its KM efforts on reducing the time needed to submit and negotiate a bid, which is of course non-billable time. They were able to reduce this time from between four and six months down to two months through giving people access to a library of bid best practices, thus reducing the non-billable overhead.

Calculating ROI

Once you have an idea of the scale of the prize, then you need to estimate the scale of the investment. The ratio of prize to investment is your ROI figure. Your investment in KM in the long term would include:

- The purchase for development cost of any new software
- Software maintenance costs
- Staffing needs and travel costs for the KM implementation program
- Staffing needs and travel costs for any central KM coordination after implementation is complete
- Staffing costs for new roles, such as community coordinator roles

Looking For Analogs

Another way to estimate the value that KM could bring to your organization is to look at case studies from other companies and use these for comparison with your own organization. In the examples the ROI is large, with return being at least 10 times the investment.

- Caterpillar claimed total savings of $75 million in the period 2003–2008 from its communities of practice, against the original investment of $2.5 million; a thirty-fold return on investment.[1]

- Shell claimed an annual value of $200 million in value from their online communities of practice, against an annual cost of $5 million.[2] ROI is therefore forty-fold.

- Siemens, in 2001,[3] claimed that their ShareNet KM system added $122 million in sales against a cost of $7.8 million; a fifteen-fold return.

- Research from the Cisco Internet Business Solutions Group showed that in fiscal year 2008 Cisco used collaboration to reduce costs by $251 million, to increase profit margin by $142 million, and to generate time savings for employees worth $380 million.[4]

- A 2002 APQC article[5] quotes the following ROI examples;

  o Chevron Texaco; Two billion dollar reduction in annual operating costs (1991 v. 1998). $670 million came from refining best practices. Total investment of more than $2 million (total figure unknown).

  o Schlumberger; $200 million cost savings, 95 percent reduction in time to resolve technical queries, 75 percent reduction in updating modifications. Total investment of approximately $20 million; a ten-fold return on investment.

  o Cap Gemini Ernst and Young. Ten-fold increase in revenue with only five-fold increase in employees.

  o IBM Global Services. 400 percent increase in service revenue. Time savings of $24 million in 1997. Approximately $750K to start up, $750K annually to maintain.

ROI Examples

Few of the public domain published KM strategies provide a Business Case or ROI, as most of these are from the public sector where ROI is less commonly used. The example below comes from the Miller, Walker, & Thompson LLP Knowledge Management: Strategic Plan[6] (for details of the ROI calculation, please refer to the referenced document).

Cost–Benefit Analysis

Before embarking on a project as substantial as a knowledge management system, it is important to perform sufficient analysis of the costs and benefits of the implementation. For this reason, I have prepared a return-on-investment calculation for MWT's project for the first year or the year in which the KMS is implemented. . . .

The Return on Investment for MWT's KMP is expected to be 13% in the first year. It is important to note that this realize is expected in the year of implementation, or the year in which the greatest number of costs are to be incurred. In the future, these costs of the KMP are expected to shrink. This return is expected to grow at a substantial rate in the following years as greater benefits, namely reductions in costs, are expected.

Additionally, at some point in the future, the firm will likely realize a growth in revenues as a result of the KMP as the KMS will create more effective and efficient processes which will lead to innovation and the expansion of operations.

Summary and Next Steps

The business case is important. The scale of the benefits determines (or justifies) the scale of the investment you are asking for. Benefits from KM can come from increasing the win ratio on bids, improving time to market or new market entry, harmonizing best practices, accelerating learning curves, reducing risk or reducing overhead. Sense check your figures against some of the available analogues.

If your business case is not mature, big, or convincing enough to gain high-level support for KM, then you may need to revert to what is known as a "guerrilla" strategy for KM, which we will describe in the following chapter.

Notes

1. Vicki Powers, "Virtual Communities at Caterpillar Foster Knowledge Sharing," June 2004, www.vickipowers.com/writings/virtual-communities.htm.

2. Laura Gibbons Paul, "How To Create A Know-It-All Company," June 13, 2007, http://www.cio.com/article/2438732/enterprise-software/how-to-create-a-know-it-all-company.html.

3. Jack Ewing, "Sharing the Wealth: How Siemens is Using Knowledge Management to Pool the Expertise of All Its Workers," BusinessWeek Online, March 19, 2001, www.providersedge.com/docs/km_articles/Sharing_the_Wealth_-_How_Siemens_is_Using_KM.pdf.

4. Cisco Systems, Inc., "Creating a Collaborative Enterprise: A Guide to Accelerating Business Value with a Collaboration Framework," 2009, http://www.cisco.com/en/US/solutions/collateral/ns340/ns856/ns870/C11-533734-00_collab_exec_guide.pdf.

5. Wesley Vestal, "Measuring Knowledge Management," American Productivity and Quality Center, August 2002, http://www.providersedge.com/docs/km_articles/measuring_km.pdf.

6. Miller, Walker, & Thompson LLP, "Knowledge Management: Strategic Plan," October 31, 2011, accessed July 11, 2014, http://incpas.org/docs/candidates-students/11butler.pdf?sfvrsn=2.

Chapter 17

The Guerrilla Strategy

All of the advice in *Designing a Successful KM Strategy*, up to this point, has assumed that you have been able to gain some level of management backing for your Knowledge Management activities; enough backing to commission you to write a strategy, and enough interest from senior managers to read and evaluate the strategy once written.

But what if you have no backing at all? What if there is nobody particularly interested in KM in your organization? What if your senior managers don't care about the topic, aren't interested in a strategy, and wouldn't read it even if it were written? In this case, much of the advice that we have provided so far—agreeing on a vision, finding the organizational drivers, selecting the critical knowledge areas, and so on—will not be very helpful to you. In some organizations it's even worse than that. In some organizations, senior managers see KM as a threat, or as tarnished goods, "something we tried in the past that failed."

In a situation like this, your only recourse is to take a strategy we call the "guerrilla KM," or "stealth KM." You have to work undercover for a while. But please don't treat this as a long-term strategy. This is a strategy for gaining support for implementation, rather than for implementation itself. There is a real limit to what you can achieve if you are trying to succeed without management support, to succeed despite a lack of leadership, or even to fight against the powers that be. The purpose of a guerrilla military unit is only to escape detection until they make a big impact on a strategic target, like a bridge or a railroad. The purpose of the stealth bomber is only to escape detection until they drop a bomb. The purpose of the guerilla knowledge manager is only to work undetected until you make a "big bang" and achieve a spectacular and strategic success.

The Guerrilla Strategy

The first step of the guerrilla KM strategy is to choose your sphere of operation. Effectively, you are looking for a KM pilot project that you can get permission to run. We talked about pilot projects in Chapter 15, and the principles for a guerrilla pilot are the same as for a normal pilot:

- You need to find a supportive manager – someone who sees the potential that KM can bring, and who already has a problem that KM can solve. If you really can't find a supportive manager, then you can be the manager, and implement KM in your own unit, but this is very much a second best approach.

- You need to be able to demonstrate and measure success in business terms. You need a clear metric, and the opportunity to make a big difference. Your pilot should not be a pilot of a technology, or approach, or a new tool; it should be a pilot of the complete KM framework in order to solve a real and important business problem.

- You need to have the potential to scale up the success so that when the pilot is over, you have not just delivered success to a supportive manager, you are bringing valuable knowledge to the rest of the organization.

- You have to have the resources to do the pilot. The resources are likely to be your own time and energy; these are not boundless and you cannot afford to fail. The guerrilla who fails vanishes without a trace.

Ken Miller, in his blog post "Guerrilla Warfare: How to Create Change When You Are Not in Charge"[1] gives some excellent additional advice:

> Focus on areas that will have high impact, high visibility and a high probability of success. Work on and dramatically

improve a system that makes everybody take notice—customers inside the organization and out, employees, and upper management. The response you want is, "How did you do that?"

Don't make the mistake of piloting the concepts on low-hanging fruit. Think big. We're not talking about moving the coffeemaker closer to the break room. If nobody notices what you've done, you've missed the point of Guerrilla Warfare. And if everybody notices what you are doing before you're done, you have also missed the point.

The second step of the guerrilla strategy is to deliver the success. Again, you need to follow the advice in *Designing a Successful KM Strategy*. Get clear on the organizational drivers within the pilot area, understand the critical knowledge, create a local framework, identify and work with the local stakeholders, and drive a change in behavior at the local level. If you have little time and little money, focus on connecting people, and on knowledge pull. Techniques such as communities of practice, peer assist, knowledge exchange, and knowledge visits can all generate a quick value return for relatively little outlay.

The third step is to publicize the success. Celebrate noisily. Put up banners, hold a party. Invite the manager to the celebration. Get the individuals involved in the pilots to tell the story of the success. Record them on video. Embed the video into presentations for senior managers. Post the video on the intranet. Write stories in the organization's magazine or newsletter. Tell the stories in external conferences. Much of guerrilla warfare is about propaganda – if nobody hears about the "big bang" then the guerrilla has failed.

Finally, you need to transform your success into high-level support. This is the point at which you start to bargain with the senior managers. Show them the local value you have created through KM, and promise them that you can scale this up across the whole organization, with little risk and high levels of return on investment. All you need from them in return are resources and support to enable you to take the next step.

A Guerrilla Strategy Requires Bravery

Sometimes people instinctively choose a guerrilla strategy to start a KM initiative because they believe it is less risky. They feel that by working undercover and out of sight, they can avoid high-level challenge; the sort of challenge that might lead to the cancellation of the KM program. However, we would recommend that instead you consider the experience of one knowledge manager, which was shared with the delegates at the KMUK conference in 2011.

This person was the head of KM at a major European company. He had been in the position for many years, and was making steady though slow progress. Then, in 2010, he had a breakthrough, resulting in the most productive year in KM he had ever had. The reason? He had lost his job.

Or, perhaps to be more exact, he was under notice that his KM post was closing.

This turned out to be a liberating experience. Released from the fear that he might lose his job (because he knew the axe had already fallen), he decided to live dangerously. Instead of waiting for permission, he acted. Instead of working through his boss, he went directly to the CEO. Things started to happen, the CEO liked what he saw, and the KM train started to accelerate. Not only that, but he was offered another KM post within the company.

The lesson from this is that if you are going to make KM work, you have to be bold. You have to live dangerously, because implementing KM, like implementing any other change process, takes courage, dedication, perseverance, and a thick skin, and it requires you to work at some very difficult conversations.

The lesson from this experience is that stealth KM, or guerrilla KM, is not necessarily the low-risk option. You will only remain below the radar as a guerrilla for as long as it takes to make the "big bang," at which point you have to come out into the open and parlay that success into a seat at the high table, and the opportunity to gain high-level support.

Then once you have the high-level support, go back to Chapter 5 of *Designing a Successful KM Strategy* and continue from there.

Summary and Next Steps

A guerrilla strategy for KM may be your only option if you have no access to high-level support. The guerrilla strategy involves working at lower levels in the organization, using whatever sponsorship you can obtain, until you have created enough evidence of value that you can make the case for higher level support. The guerrilla strategy is not easy, and requires bravery; the purpose of a guerrilla strategy is to provoke attention, not to hide out of sight.

The guerrilla strategy is not the only special-case strategy, and in Chapter 18 we will look at another special case: the knowledge retention strategy.

Note

1. Ken Miller, "Guerilla [*sic*] Warfare: How to Create Change When You Are Not in Charge," Public Great, May 1, 2009, http://kenmillerblog.info/2009/05/guerilla-warfare/.

A Retention-Based Knowledge Management Strategy

Many Western engineering-based, manufacturing, and utility companies face an imminent and potentially catastrophic crisis. This is highlighted as follows in a study from a utility company.[1]

- The average U.S. utility worker is 44 years old, and the average U.S. craft worker is 50. (Average U.S. worker is 37.)

- Within 4 years, as many as 60 percent of today's experienced workers will retire

- The shrinking labor force leads to an increased competition for talent

- 80 percent of utility industry HR Executives identified the aging work force as their biggest worry

- Less than half have a strategy in place to deal with this problem.

The figures are typical. It is estimated[2] that more than a quarter of the U.S. working population will retire in the next 5 years, while in the United Kingdom, people belonging to the 45- to 59-years-old range will soon constitute the majority of the active workforce. Highly strategic and knowledge intensive jobs are mostly filled by baby boomers who will be heading for retirement in the near future. If nothing is done, the knowledge they hold in their heads will leave with them, and the capability of the organization will slip away. Industry is racing toward a demographic cliff-edge, and Knowledge Management will provide the only parachute.

If your organization is in a situation like this, then it is quite possible that your KM Strategy will focus on one issue only, namely knowledge retention and transfer.

This is a special case of KM Strategy, and so merits a chapter on its own. This strategy takes an organization-focused look at the risk and the urgency, prioritizes topics and individuals for retention activities, and puts in place a planned and monitored approach to retaining and transferring the knowledge to new and younger staff. The components of the strategy follow.

Business Driver

In Chapter 6 we discussed a number of business drivers for KM. A retention strategy has only one business driver: risk reduction. If nothing is done to retain and transfer knowledge, then the organization faces a steady decrease in competence and a steady increase in business risk. An example of the risk of knowledge loss is shown in this story from the Aberdeen Press and Journal[3].

> When Boeing offered early retirement to 9,000 senior employees, an unexpected rush of new commercial airplane orders left the company critically short of skilled production workers.
>
> The knowledge lost from veteran employees, combined with the inexperience of their replacements, threw the firm's 737 and 747 assembly lines into chaos. Overtime skyrocketed and workers were chasing planes along the line to finish assembly.
>
> Management finally had to shut down production for more than three weeks to straighten out the assembly process, which forced Boeing to take a $1.6 billion charge against earnings and contributed to an eventual management shake-up.

Although this story refers to a planned retirement, and represents an extreme case, unplanned retirements and resignations can also constitute a real business risk if business-critical knowledge is held in the heads of a few experts.

Scope and Vision

The scope of your strategy should cover all of the jobs and all of the functions within the organization where there is significant risk of knowledge loss; in other words where the workforce is approaching retirement age. The vision might be something like this:

"Effective and smooth transfer of knowledge from retiring experts, so that the business suffers no loss and no added business risk as the experts retire."

Critical Knowledge Areas and Assessment of the Current State

A key stage in preparing a knowledge retention strategy is to map out the scale and urgency of the problem (refer to Chapters 8 and 9 for more coverage). This scan can take place in one of two dimensions:

- A scan of the knowledge topics, characterizing them by attributes such as criticality, the level of documentation, the level of spread within the organization, and the risk of loss.
- A scan of the individuals, characterizing them by the knowledge they hold, and the imminence of their departure.

Choose the first option for large organizations, where there are more topics than individuals, and the second option for companies with 100 staff or less. Whichever option you choose, the result of the scan will be a map of the organizational knowledge, identifying those areas where the risk of loss is highest, the consequence of that risk is greatest, and the need to act is most urgent. This allows a high grading of the areas for retention activity.

It is those high-graded areas that represent the critical knowledge areas within the strategy, and which will prioritize your efforts in the short term.

KM Framework

The knowledge retention strategy is an unusual strategy in that it is largely driven by urgency. The KM framework that you apply depends on the circumstances and specifically how much time you have available. The strategy is driven by triage as much as by anything else.

Plot each of the high-graded retention areas on the Boston Square shown in Figure 18.1. The two axes to this square are the time it will take to transfer the knowledge, and the time available for transfer.

Where the time needed to transfer knowledge exceeds the available time (top left quadrant on Figure 18.1), the retention program is in reactive mode, and the focus is on capturing as much knowledge as possible while there is still time. The departing expert works with interviewers and knowledge capture staff to ensure that the most valuable knowledge is captured and documented.

Where the time needed to transfer knowledge matches the available time (top right and bottom left quadrants), the focus is on both capture and transfer, and the departing experts work with their replacements,

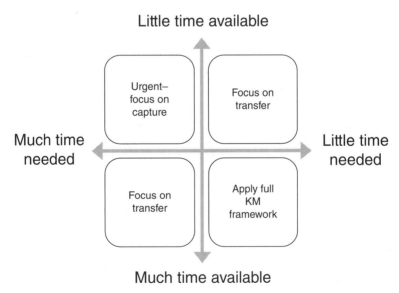

Figure 18.1   Triage plot

through coaching and mentoring and through interviewing, at the same time as documenting the crucial knowledge.

Where the time available is significant (bottom right quadrant) a departing expert can be involved in a wider KM role, ideally as the leader of a community of practice and the owner of a knowledge asset. Knowledge can be captured and transferred as part of his or her normal job, thus reducing the risk of knowledge loss. If your critical knowledge plots in the bottom right quadrant, you don't need a specific knowledge retention strategy; you need a full KM strategy.

In each case, there are the additional options of replacing the expert with somebody equally experienced, or of removing the need for that expertise. For example, if the only person who knows how to operate a particular software program is leaving, then maybe the cheapest and most effective solution would be to replace the software program.

Regardless of the reason for the knowledge retention strategy, you need to do a lot of knowledge capture. If the knowledge is not captured but rather is only transferred from one head to another, then you are merely postponing the risk of loss. We recommend that the more junior staff lead the knowledge transfer exercise, capture the knowledge, and structure it within a knowledge repository so that it is available to them and their colleagues in the future. Using the juniors to capture the knowledge removes some of the burden from the experts, and allows the experts to check, through reviewing the captured knowledge, whether the juniors fully understand the transferred knowledge. The documented knowledge needs to be stored in a wiki, portal, or other knowledge base, which can be owned by the relevant community of practice and kept populated, alive, and up to date.

Stakeholders

Once triage analysis is complete, the stakeholders can be identified (see Chapter 14). Stakeholders usually include the following;

- Managers of the business units with the greatest risk of retention loss
- Departing experts

- Successors to the departing experts
- Communities of practice in the areas of expertise
- Human Resources department

One of your key stakeholder groupings will be the people within the organization who have clear accountability for the retention and transfer process. Depending on the situation, this can lie with the relevant supervisor or manager, with the functional leadership (chief engineer, head of maintenance, etc.), with the HR department, or with the KM team.

Change Management

A retention exercise is, in many cases, a reactive stopgap measure to cover a specific risk, and does not have the same culture change overtones that many other KM strategies do. However, there will be an element of change management (discussed in detail in Chapter 13) and communication in the way you deal with the stakeholders, and in any retention exercise requiring extensive knowledge transfer the people involved in the transfer will need to be trained in the skills of knowledge harvesting, interviewing, and knowledge packaging. Similarly the departing experts will need an introduction to coaching and mentoring skills.

Piloting

Selecting a pilot (as detailed in Chapter 15) within a retention strategy should be relatively straightforward; you find the most urgent and important knowledge retention issue with the most cooperative people involved, and start there.

Governance of the Strategy

You will need an element of governance in your strategy, so that you can be sure knowledge retention and transfer are proceeding as planned. The owner of the retention and transfer process works with the departing expert, and with the successor (if available), to create a detailed plan for knowledge capture and transfer. The plan is owned by the owner, the expert, and his/her successor, and represents a series of activities including knowledge capture, documentation, mentoring, training, and coaching. Each knowledge topic, or each departing individual, is covered by a single plan.

During the retention and transfer activities, the plans are monitored and the situation is reported to management through a retention dashboard. Management can therefore be reassured that the risk of knowledge loss is being fully and effectively addressed.

Example

An interesting example of a knowledge retention strategy is offered by the Los Angeles Bureau of Sanitation[4].

In this document, the priority individuals were identified through a cross-plot of age and tenure as shown in Figure 18.2. Those individuals aged 50 or older, with more than 20 years tenure, were chosen as the high priority area.

A second step was to identify individual personnel through a series of focus groups and a survey of Bureau division managers. Each division

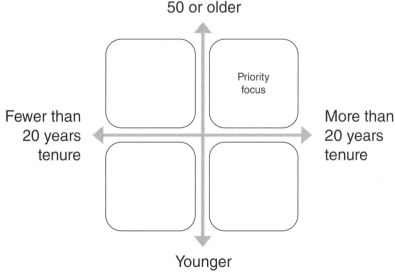

Figure 18.2   High grading staff by tenure and age

manager was asked to identify the top three people in their division who, if they were to leave the Bureau, would severely impact its operations.

Finally the most critical knowledge areas, for highest priority attention, were identified as follows:

- Enhancing Bureau knowledge of the collection system

- Troubleshooting of wastewater treatment facilities

- How natural disasters (e.g., earthquakes) have been handled in the past.

For each of these areas, the Bureau developed a KM framework based on the following four elements:

- Human resource policies and procedures

- Knowledge transfer practices

- Information technology applications to capture, store, and share knowledge

- Knowledge recovery initiatives

Summary and Next Steps

A retention-based KM strategy may be appropriate in certain cases, where the business imperative is driven solely by the risk of knowledge loss as experienced staff retire. The strategy involves identifying the critical knowledge areas at greatest risk of loss, and applying a triage approach to identify whether to focus on capture, transfer, or a complete KM framework.

Once your strategy is complete, whether it is a full strategy, a guerrilla strategy, or a retention strategy, start preparing for the next steps by putting the delivery organization in place, as described in Chapter 19.

Notes

1. Dick Brabham, "TVA's Approach to Knowledge Retention: Learning from Our Mistakes," August 2009 presentation, accessed July 9, 2014, http://www.tva.gov/knowledgeretention/pdf/tvppa_aug09.pdf.

2.   Jeanne C. Meister, "Addressing the Perils of Lost Knowledge and an Aging Work-force," *Chief Learning Officer* 4, no. 3 (March 2005): 28.

3.   Jeremy Cresswell, "The Not-So-Hidden Cost of Lost Knowledge." *Aberdeen Press and Journal*, September 1, 2008.

4.   Margaret Umphres, Varouj Abkian, and Charles Turhollow, "A Knowledge Reten-tion Strategy for the Los Angeles Bureau of Sanitation," in *2007 AWWA/WEF Joint Management Conference Proceedings* (American Water Works Association, 2007).

CHAPTER **19**

Building the Implementation Team

Once you have drafted your Knowledge Management (KM) strategy, presented it to senior managers, and have been given the go-ahead to proceed, what happens next? *Designing a Successful KM Strategy* is not a guide to KM implementation and delivery (that would be an entire book in its own right), but in this chapter we will help you with the next step by recommending how your implementation team and organization should be structured.

Once your KM strategy has been submitted to management and you have received approval to proceed, you need to:

- Appoint the KM team leader
- Appoint the KM team
- Determine reporting lines for the KM team
- Appoint the steering team
- Plan the implementation

More detail on each of these steps follows.

Appointing the KM Team Leader

A leader for the KM program may already have been appointed. If you are creating the KM strategy document, this may in fact be your role However, let's think for a moment about the ideal characteristics of a

KM team leader (if you don't possess these characteristics yourself, you may prefer to play a supporting role, perhaps as knowledge manager for the KM team) The characteristics of the leader are among the key indicators of success of the KM program We have seen several KM initiatives fail because the wrong leader was chosen, and others succeed through excellent leadership.

First and foremost, the leader must be a change agent—a visionary, with drive, focus, and creativity. The leader will need to initiate action and activity with enthusiasm, and not to try to hold onto KM; it has to be passed on to others for them to take the KM baton and run forward with it. The leader needs to be the agent and driver of change and the initiator of change in others.

Additionally, the leader needs cross functional skills and influencing skills. Influencing is critical; the leader needs to influence other people who are not in the KM team such as the key stakeholders in the organization.

The leader needs a strong profile in the organization. He or she needs to be an insider who knows the organization, the way it is structured, the language and jargon that is used, and the stories that are told. In particular the leader needs to know the people within the organization and to be very well networked.

If you can't get an insider to play this role, you will need to hire someone with strong interpersonal skills, excellent communication and listening skills, and the ability to quickly understand what the issues are in an area.

Above all, the leader needs to be able to translate KM into the day-to-day working language of the organization. The key word here is "translate." The KM leader, and indeed any KM professional, needs a grounding in KM theory and concepts, and is perfectly entitled to use the jargon and the technical terms when planning, designing and delivering a KM approach. But that jargon and dogma has to stop when you reach the internal customer. Here's what a knowledge manager said to us recently:

> I would be suspicious of any KM leader using KM terminology. I would like to hear business and customer

terminology. When queried and challenged on that, then they can explain it in a KM way. To me, that would suggest they understand the customer, and they understand KM and how to apply it to the customer and vice versa.

Finally, the leader needs patience. Lots of patience! The leader needs to be in KM for the long haul.

Appointing the KM Team

Once you have the leader of the KM team in place, you need to appoint the rest of the team. As we explained in Chapter 9, three of the enabling elements of KM are people, process, and technology; you need people on the KM team who can address these three elements. You will need people skills, you will need process skills, and you will need technology skills.

People Skills

Coaching and training skills are some of the core "people skills" needed by KM team members. The aim of the KM team is to introduce new behaviors, new practices, new roles and new accountabilities to the organization, and so the team will need people skilled in training, coaching, and mentoring. Look for people with skills as change agents and business coaches. It is likely that one or more people with a training background will be on the team.

Facilitation/influencing skills are also important. The KM implementation team has a hard job ahead of it, changing the behaviors and ultimately the culture of the organization. They will be working very closely with people, often skeptical people, and they will need superior influencing and facilitation skills. Secure facilitation training for the KM team members if they need it.

Finally, you will need somebody on the team with marketing and communication skills. The early stages of implementing KM are all about raising awareness, and selling the idea. The KM team needs at least one person who is skilled at presenting and marketing, and who can manage and deliver against the communications strategy, as part of the change management described in Chapter 13.

Writing skills are also important. The processes of knowledge capture and packaging are in some ways akin to journalism. Interviewing, group interviewing (e.g. retrospects), analysis, summary, write-up, and presentation are all part of the stock-in-trade of journalists and knowledge managers alike. Make sure there is at least one person on the team with journalistic or technical writing skills, and preferably more than one.

Process Skills

The members of the KM team will also need to be skilled in, or at least familiar with, the operational processes of the organization. The organizational backgrounds of the core team need to be varied. The KM team will be attempting to change behavior, and to embed KM into the operational processes across a large part of, if not the entire, organization, and therefore the team should contain people with experience and skills in each major organizational subdivision. Certainly, during the piloting stage you need people who understand the organizational areas in which the pilots will take place.

Having people in the team with a business background helps to establish the credibility of the team. When members of the KM team are working with organizational projects, they want to be seen as part of the organizational team, not specialists from the head office who might know very little about operations. Team members must speak the language of the organization, both the technical language and the operational language, in order to help the leader translate the KM concepts into operational processes.

Technology Skills

The KM team needs at least one person who has strengths in the details of the current in-house technology, understands the potential of new technology as an enabler for KM, and can help define the most appropriate technologies to introduce to the organization. Technology is one of the main enablers, and you will need to analyze the current status of the KM technology and select additional technologies to fill any gaps. Chapter 12 discusses the work you may need to undertake to align the KM technology, so ensure you have the right skills on the team to do this work.

Passion

The members of the team should be passionate about Knowledge Management and the benefit it can bring. Team members must be seen to be personally committed to KM if they are to retain credibility. They need training in KM theory and practice, and access to books, conferences and forums on the topic.

Finding such people is not easy, but changing the culture of an organization is not easy either. Without the right people on the team, you will never get the right result, even with the best consultants in the world to support you. However, with the right team, the right leader, and the right approach, absolutely anything can be done, and KM implementation will be, if not easy, at least straightforward and successful.

Deciding the Reporting Lines

Should KM sit within HR? IT? Somewhere else?

KM, as we discussed in Chapter 4 and again in Chapter 9, involves attention to four things, people, process, technology, and governance, which form one dimension of your KM framework. Each of these four elements is vital, and each links to, and is supported by, other parts of the organization as follows:

- The people aspect is linked to HR, as new roles and account-abilities will need to be created, together with new career paths and recognition schemes

- The technology aspect is linked to IT, as new applications, systems, and (sometimes) hardware need to be in place

- The process aspect needs to be linked to Operations, as new processes have to be embedded into the operational workflow

- The governance aspect needs to be linked to the top management, as their support, involvement, and drive from the top is vital

These four elements need to be in balance. Generally, if any one of these supporting departments is "in charge" of KM, the balance becomes distorted—not because of any negative intent, but just by the nature and the natural way of thinking of the people within that department. Consider these risks:

- KM that reports to the IT department risks focusing too heavily on technology

- KM that reports to the HR department tends to focus too heavily on people-related interventions such as communities of practice, coaching, and training

- KM that reports to operations tends to focus too heavily on operational process

- KM that reports to the governance body tends to focus too much on policies

What's the answer? The answer is to run KM as a cross-functional, separate small department, independent of these four, but to involve the heads of all four supporting departments on a KM steering team or steering committee, as these will be four of your most important stakeholders.

The Steering Team

Any time we kick off a KM program with a client, we recommend that they put together a steering team, or steering committee, to help steer the program. This is the mechanism that keeps KM tightly aligned to the needs of the business. The leader of the KM team does not report to the steering team; he or she reports to a high-level sponsor in the sponsoring department, and the steering team acts to advise both the sponsor and the KM team leader.

We have already introduced the idea of a steering team in Chapters 4, 13, and 14, and once the strategy has been approved, it's time to convene the steering team. Select between 6 and 10 people in total, such as:

- The head of HR and/or the head of Learning and Development, to cover the people aspect

- Senior people in the main activity areas such as the head of Marketing, the Chief Engineer, or the head of the Project Office, to cover process aspects

- The CIO, CTO or the Vice President of Technology to cover the technology aspect

- The Head of Strategy or Head of Planning to cover governance aspects

- The sponsor of the KM program, to act as chair of the team

- Other high-level stakeholders identified through the stakeholder analysis discussed in Chapter 14

The purpose of the steering team is to:

- Provide a source of additional input and insight from people outside the core KM team to ensure the team doesn't become introverted and lose their business-led outlook

- Provide a source of rigorous challenge when needed (in a safe environment)

- Further build and maintain the profile of KM

- Bring influential thought leaders closer to the KM program

- Help the KM team to see emerging risks and opportunities

Implementation Planning

Once the KM strategy and team are both in place, it's time to build the plan. You already have the pilots identified, you know what's missing in your framework that needs to be put in place, and you have a communications strategy and plan already crafted. You know the stakeholders to influence, the departments to work with, and the key people who need to be on-side. Now plan out the steps that you need to take, put them in a timeline, and estimate the required resources.

Start with your agreed technology roadmap, your agreed pilots, and your change management plan. Write out each step or task you need to do on a sticky note, together with an estimate of the resource you will need (the number of people-days, the cost of technology or travel), and put these notes onto a large, clear wall in order to start building the plan.

Your plan will probably include the following activities:

- Management of change, including communication, training, and awareness-raising activities

- Stakeholder interactions (reporting and review)

- KM piloting

- Developing baseline metrics and KPIs (key performance indicators)

- Technology requirements analysis

- Documented knowledge lifecycle process

- Developing a high-level taxonomy and metadata

- Roles and responsibilities definitions

- Coaching of staff with KM roles

- Process definition

- Process testing

- Review and endorsement of the piloted framework

- Governance definition

- Development of training and reference material

- Development of a roadmap for roll-out of the KM framework within the organization; including training

- Updating existing policies and standards to include the KM elements

Once the plan looks reasonable and the activities are placed in a logical order, transfer the tasks and resource estimates to a spreadsheet or project planning software and start to add up the resources and the cost, adjusting the timing of the various tasks to smooth out the resource load. This is where you will truly begin to appreciate the magnitude of the implementation task and the resources you will need in order to be successful.

The finalization of the plan typically includes a maximum of two iterations involving review sessions with identified stakeholders; more than two iterations results in loss of momentum and loss of interest by the stakeholders. Reviewing the strategic plan with the stakeholders and getting input helps with buy-in and support, and also ensures that nothing has been misunderstood or overlooked.

Budgeting

With the plan comes the budget. Each step within the plan can be estimated in terms of the cost of human resources and technology. Add overhead. If your organization operates in many countries, assume that you will do a significant amount of travel and designate time and resources for training, reporting, and answering requests from the organization. Check the budget to see whether the four elements of people, process, technology, and governance all have a representative portion of the budget. If 90 percent of the budget is going to technology, for example, you have severely underestimated the other three elements.

Enjoy this step. If your strategy is sound and you have the support you need from the top and the right people on the team, then moving from strategy to tactics should be relatively straightforward.

Summary

This chapter has taken you through the next steps following completion of your strategy, including appointing the KM team and team leader, setting up the steering team, and planning the implementation. From here on, you're on your own, and the work of this book is done. That said, if you have followed the advice within *Designing a Successful KM Strategy*, then you have laid the best possible foundation for your KM program, and can move forward with confidence.

CHAPTER **20**

Final Words

For all the tools and technologies and nuances, and all the things we do to complicate KM, at its heart it is about making sure that the decision makers at all levels in the organization have access to the crucial knowledge they need to make the right decisions. Then it's about making sure that the correct roles, processes, technology, and governance are in place, to identify, capture, and transfer that organizational knowledge. Finally, it's about change management, and changing to a culture where knowledge is an important asset.

The change management aspect of KM involves the hardest work. There is great technology out there, well-defined processes that work extremely well, an understanding of the roles and skill sets needed, and there's a good understanding of the governance elements. All of that is easy enough. It's the strategic change that's difficult, and that's where organizations most often go wrong with their KM programs. They do the easy stuff, not the hard stuff. They buy the technologies, they print the booklets, they work with the enthusiasts and sing with the choir, but without a firm strategic grounding and a good change management approach, they don't deliver KM's full potential.

By following the advice presented in *Designing a Successful KM Strategy*, you will avoid this pitfall.

Creating your strategy will allow you to have the vital discussions with the CEO and the senior management team about the value KM can deliver to the organization, the business drivers it should be aligned with, the critical knowledge that needs to be addressed, the change that needs to be in place, the stakeholders who need to be engaged, and

187

the top business pilot areas where you should make a start. Your strategy document will be a record of those discussions, and will provide a secure basis for the work ahead.

Your strategy will be your key reference document when the hard work of change begins; when it is time to tussle with the hard-pressed team leaders and work out what you can do to help them, and what they can do to help you, to get out and work in detail with the pilot projects, and to deliver the spectacular successes that will act as a beacon to the rest of the organization. Your strategy will also help you engage the skeptics and the doubters and the people who are "just too busy" for KM.

Your strategy will help you avoid leading one of the 80 percent of KM programs that fail, by defining your vision, objectives, and principles, and ensuring your KM program is fully driven by the organizational needs. It will be a public record of your agreement with top management about the direction KM will take and the areas on which to focus. It will define the scope of your KM operations, and help you avoid squandering precious resources.

Your strategy is the first and most important step on a successful KM journey. Good luck, and enjoy the ride!

Appendix A: Communication Plan Template

Part 1 - Communication until the first success

Target Audience	Message	Medium	Frequency	Accountability	Approval
Steering Group					
Senior Managers					
Stakeholder Grouping A					
Stakeholder Grouping B					
Stakeholder Grouping C					
All Staff					

Part 2 - Communication of successes during trials and piloting

Target Audience	Message	Medium	Frequency	Accountability	Approval
Steering Group					
Senior Managers					
Stakeholder Grouping A					
Stakeholder Grouping B					
Stakeholder Grouping C					
All Staff					

Part 3 - Communication during roll-out and training

Target Audience	Message	Medium	Frequency	Accountability	Approval
Steering Group					
Senior Managers					
Stakeholder Grouping A					
Stakeholder Grouping B					
Stakeholder Grouping C					
All Staff					

About the Authors

Stephanie Barnes has over 20 years of successful experience in KM and accounting in the high technology, health care, and public accounting sectors. She is currently a Knowledge Management consultant at Missing Puzzle Piece Consulting, where she focuses on aligning people, process, and technology. She works with clients in financial and professional services, as well as in the high-tech industry and the non-profit sector, among others. She has been doing KM work for more than 14 years and is the Knoco Ltd. franchisee for Canada.

Stephanie graduated from Brock University with a BBA in Accounting and from McMaster University with an MBA in Information Technology. She is ITIL Masters certified as well as having a Business Systems Analysis certificate. In May 2011, Ark Group published Stephanie's report, "Aligning People, Process, and Technology in Knowledge Management."

Stephanie can be found on the web at www.missingpuzzlepiece consulting.ca, on Twitter @MPuzzlePiece, on Slideshare at http://www .slideshare.net/stephaniebarnes/, and on LinkedIn at http://ca.linkedin .com/in/stephanieabarnes/.

Dr. Nick Milton is director and co-founder of Knoco Ltd., with over 21 years working in Knowledge Management. At Knoco, Nick has helped develop and deliver KM strategies, implementation programs, and KM services in a wide range of different organizations around the globe. He has a particular interest in Lessons Learned programs, and has managed major lessons capture programs, particularly in the area of mergers & acquisitions and high technology engineering. He is the author of *The Lessons Learned Handbook* (Woodhead Publishing, 2010) and *Knowledge Management for Teams and Projects* (Chandos Publishing, 2005), and co-author of *Knowledge Management for Sales and Marketing* (Chandos Publishing, 2011) and *Performance Through Learning—Knowledge Management in Practice* (Elsevier, 2004).

Prior to founding Knoco, Nick spent two years at the center of the team that made BP the leading KM company in the world, acting as the team knowledge manager, developing and implementing BP's knowledge of "how to manage knowledge" and coordinating the BP KM Community of Practice.

Nick blogs most days at nickmilton.com and can be found on Twitter @nickknoco. He lives near Bath, UK.

Index